New Paradigms Original Audio 1995
Book Version Plus Extra Chapters 2021 ©
Authored by Bob Proctor & Michele Blood

Published by MusiVation Int'l LLC
PO Box 12933
La Jolla, California 92039
USA
All rights reserved.
Printed in the United States of America
ISBN: 978-1-890679-86-6

This book may not be copied, duplicated or used in any way without the written permission of the publishers.

For wholesale copies

email team@TheMysticalExperience.com

Cover art by Michele Blood and Bob Proctor
1995™

Table of Contents

Introduction 1
Decision 3
Success 23
Communication 39
Risk 59
Persistence 81
Action 100
The Power of Meditation 117
Intuition 124

Introduction

Hi, this is Michele Blood. I am so excited and I'm very happy for you because you have made a decision. A decision to change your life to the positive. How are you going to change your life to the positive? By changing your thinking, changing your paradigm. What is a paradigm? A paradigm is simply your subconscious thinking, thoughts, feelings, and actions from the past. It is your subconscious mind.

Now to change your life to the positive we must feed ourselves new thoughts so that in our subconscious mind we have a new paradigm. This book consists of transcriptions from New Paradigms, the New Paradigms audio program that Bob Proctor and I wrote and recorded in Kuala Lumpur back in 1995. I have also added some extra chapters for you to begin to go deeper into consciousness. You are going to learn about so many wonderful topics and gain clarity on areas of your life that haven't quite been brought into harmony. Perhaps you weren't sure about how to move ahead. Today you are going to move ahead. And on Chapter One you are going to learn about how to make great Decisions and so much more. It is powerful to read these words over and over again. These messages truly raise consciousness fast!

You have also received in this program the audio recordings and all of the Affirmation Power Music Songs. We recommend that you listen to all the programs and then listen to all the affirmation, positive songs. We suggest for you to listen to a different audio every day for 90 days. Now when you've gone through the whole New Paradigms Program including this book what we'd like you to do is whenever you feel a shift happening and you're going back into say a lower oscillation of energy and you want to get up into a positive frame of mind listen to all of them again. If you have a decision to make, put on the Decision tape. If you feel that you're not really in synergy, listen to the Synergy song, and always remember that you can do it. We all have the same God-given potential. We all have been given the greatest gift that life can give us, and that gift is the power to think and love.

So, welcome to New Paradigms.

If you have this print book and you would love to have the complete audiobook version you can go to the following link to get the New Paradigms audiobook at a discount. Just go to:
www.NewParadigmsAudio.com

On the checkout page click the link that says "Have a coupon? Click here to enter your code" and enter the following coupon code on the checkout page.

More Love *(Is the code)*

Decision

There's a single mental mood you can make which in a millisecond will solve enormous problems for you. It has the potential to improve almost any personal or business situation you will ever encounter. And it can literally propel you down the path to incredible success. We have a name for this magic mental activity. It is called DECISION!

TheMysticalExperience.com/NPSongs

The world's most successful people share a common quality. They make decisions. Yes, decision-makers go to the top, and those who do not make decisions seem to go nowhere. Think about it. Decisions or the lack of them are responsible for the breaking or making of careers.

Individuals who have become very proficient in making decisions without being influenced by the opinions of others are the same people whose annual income falls into the six and seven-figure categories. The person who has never developed the mental strength to make these vital moves is relegated to the lower income ranks all of their commercial career. And more often than not their life becomes little more than a dull, boring existence. It's not just your income that is affected by decisions. Your whole life is dominated by this power. The health of your mind and body, the well-being of your family, your social life, the type of relationships you develop, are all dependent upon your ability to make sound decisions.

You would think anything as important as Decision making, when it has such far-reaching power, would be taught in every school, but it's not. And to compound the problem, decision-making is not only missing from the curriculum of almost all of our formal educational institutions, it has been left out of virtually all of the training and human resource development programs in our corporate world. At this point, you could be asking yourself, "How is a person expected to develop this mental ability?" Well, I have the answer for you. You must do it on your own. And you've already begun by thinking about and digesting the information that I am sharing with you. This message is causing you to become more aware of the importance of decisions.

There's an excellent book that I found on a trip to Malaysia which you might want to add to your library. It has some very powerful information between the covers. It's called "Decision Power" by Harvey Kaye. It's published by Prentice Hall. Kaye's book has a subtitle, "How To Make Decisions With Confidence." That's the only way to make decisions. Don't make your decisions and then worry about whether you're doing the right thing. It is important to understand that it's not difficult to learn how to make wise decisions. With the proper information and by subjecting yourself to certain disciplines you can become a very proficient and effective decision-maker. And remember, it is the people who do become effective at decision-making who receive a big share of the world's rewards.

Decision-making is definitely a worthwhile subject to study and a mental discipline you can master. Decision-making could be compared to a number of other mental disciplines like thinking, imagineering, or concentrating. Each one, when developed, brings with it tremendous rewards. The person who makes the decision to strengthen these mental muscles receives as their reward what is often considered a charmed life. You can virtually eliminate conflict and confusion in your life by becoming proficient at making decisions. Decision-making brings order to your mind. And of course, this order is then reflected in your objective world, your results. James Allen, the great Victorian author, might have been thinking of decisions when he wrote, "We think in secret, and it comes to pass. Environment is but our looking glass."

No one can see you making decisions, but they will almost always see the results of your decisions. The person who fails to develop this ability to make decisions is doomed because indecision sets up internal conflicts which can, without warning, escalate to all-out mental and emotional wars. Psychiatrists have a name to describe these internal wars, it is ambivalence.

My Oxford dictionary tells me that ambivalence is "The coexistence in one person of opposite feelings toward the same objective." You do not have to be the brightest person in town, and you certainly do not require a doctor's degree in Psychiatry to understand you are going to have a bit of difficulty in your life by permitting your mind to remain in an ambivalent state for any period of time.

The person who does permit it to exist will become very despondent and virtually incapable of any type of productive activity. It is obvious that anyone who finds themselves in such a mental state is not living; at best they are merely existing. A decision or a series of decisions would change everything. A very basic law of the universe is "Create or Disintegrate." Indecision causes disintegration. How often have you heard a person say, "I don't know what to do?" How often have you heard yourself say, "What should I do?" Think about some of the indecisive feelings you and virtually everyone else on this planet experience from time to time. Love them/Leave them. Quit/Stay.

Do it/Don't do it. Go bankrupt/No don't. Go to work/Watch TV. Buy it/Don't buy it. Say it/Don't say it. Tell them/Don't tell them.

Everyone, on occasion, has experienced these feelings of ambivalence. If it happens to you frequently decide right now to stop it. The cause of ambivalence is indecision, but we must keep in mind that the truth is not always in the appearance of things. Indecision is a cause of ambivalence however it is a secondary cause. It is not the primary cause. I have been studying the behavior of people who have become very proficient at making decisions for over a quarter-century. They all have one thing in common. They have a very strong self-image, a high degree of self-esteem. They may be as different as night is to day in numerous other respects but they certainly possess confidence.

Low self-esteem or a lack of confidence is the real culprit here. Decision-makers are not afraid of making an error. If and when they make an error in their decision or fail at something, they have the ability to shrug it off. They learn from the experience, but they never submit to failure. Every decision-maker was either fortunate enough to have been raised in an environment where decision-making was a part of their upbringing, or they developed the ability themselves at a later date. They are aware of something that everyone who hopes to live a full life must understand. Decision-making is something you cannot avoid.

That is certainly worth repeating, if you hope to live a full life you must become a proficient decision-maker. I might also add that even those who are proficient at making decisions know they can improve. You may be thinking, "All right. Where do I start?" You start improving your ability to make decisions in exactly the same place you start any journey and with exactly the same resources. You decide. Start right where you are with whatever you've got.

That is the cardinal principle of decision-making. Decide right where you are with whatever you've got. That is precisely why most people never master this important aspect of life. They permit their resources to dictate if and when a Decision will or can be made. When John Kennedy asked Wernher Von Braun what it would take to build a rocket that would carry a man to the moon and return him safely to earth his answer was simple and direct, "The will to do it." President Kennedy never asked if it was possible. He never asked if they could afford it or any one of a thousand other questions, all of which would have at the time been valid questions.

President Kennedy made a Decision. He said, "We will put a man on the moon and return him safely to Earth before the end of the decade." The fact that it had never been done before in all of the hundreds of thousands of years of human history was not even a consideration. He decided where he was with what he had. The objective was accomplished in his mind the second he made the Decision. It was only a matter of time which is governed by the natural law of the universe before the goal was manifested in form for the whole world to see.

I was just hours ago, in an office with three people. We were discussing the purchase of shares in a company. I was selling, they were buying. After a reasonable amount of time, one of the partners asked me when I wanted a Decision. I replied, "Right now." I said, "You already know what you want to do." There was some discussion about money. I pointed out that money had nothing to do with it. Once you make the Decision, you'll find the money every time.

If that is the only benefit you receive from this particular message on Decision burn it into your mind. It will change your life. I explain to these two people that I never let money enter my mind when I'm deciding whether I will or will not do something. Whether I can afford it or not is never a consideration. Whether I want it or not is the only consideration. You can afford anything. There is an infinite supply of money.

All of the money in the world is available to you when the Decision is firmly made. If you need the money you will attract it.

I am well aware there are any number of people who will say, "This is absurd. You can't just decide to do something if you do not have the necessary resources." And that's fine if that's the way they choose to think. I see that as a very limiting way of thinking. In truth, it is probably not thinking at all. It is very likely an opinion being expressed that was inherited from an older member of their family who did not think either. Thinking is very important. Decision-makers are great thinkers.

Do you ever give much consideration to your thoughts? How do they affect the various aspects of your life? Although this should be one of our most serious considerations, unfortunately for many people it is not. There's a very small, select few who make any attempt to control or govern their thoughts. Anyone who has made a study of the great thinkers, the decision-makers, the achievers of history, will know they very rarely agreed on anything when it comes to a study of human life.

However, there was one point which they were in complete and unanimous agreement on, and that was that we become what we think about. What do you think about? Listen again, this time very carefully to the lyrics of this song as Michele shares them with you.

Decision Lyrics

Decision
Decision Decision Decision

Winners make decisions fast
Losers make them slow
Winning is a choice just decide and go

Decision
Decision Decision Decision

Make Decisions be decisive
Show the world you're bold
You'll be loved you'll be admired
You'll attract your share of gold

Isn't that great? Isn't she great? You've got to order all of Michele's albums on Affirmation Power. They're phenomenal. Her positive songs will keep your thoughts on the right track. You and I must realize that our thoughts ultimately control every Decision we make. You are the sum total of your thoughts. By taking charge this very minute you can guarantee yourself a good day. Refuse to let unhappy, negative people or circumstances affect you.

The greatest stumbling block you will ever encounter when making important decisions in your life is circumstance. We let circumstance get us off the hook when we should be giving it everything we've got. More dreams are shattered, and goals lost because of circumstance than any other single factor. How often have you caught yourself saying, "I'd like to do this or that, but I can't because..." Whatever follows 'because' is the circumstance. Circumstance may cause a detour in your life, but you should never permit them to stop you from making important decisions. Napoleon said, "Circumstance. I make them."

The next time you hear someone say they would like to vacation in Paris or purchase a particular automobile, but they can't because they have no money, explain they don't need the money until they make a Decision to go to Paris or purchase the car. When the decision is made, they will figure out a way to get the amount needed. They always do. Many misguided individuals try something once or twice and if they do not hit the bullseye, they feel they are a failure. Failing does not make anyone a failure but quitting most certainly does and quitting is a Decision. By following that form of reason, you would have to say when you make a Decision to quit you make a Decision to fail.

Every day in America you will hear about a baseball player signing a contract that will pay him a few million dollars a year. You should try and keep in mind that same player misses the ball more often than he hits it when he steps up to the plate. Everyone remembers Babe Ruth for the 714 home runs he hit, but they very rarely mention that he struck out 1330 times. Charles F. Kettering said, and I quote, "When you're inventing if you flunk 999 times and succeed once you're in."

Now that is true of just about any activity you can name. The world will soon forget your failures in light of your achievements. Don't worry about failing. It will toughen you up and get you ready for the big win. Winning is a Decision. Many years ago, Helen Keller was asked if she thought there was anything worse than being blind. She quickly replied there was something much worse. She said, "The most pathetic person in the world is the person who has their sight but no vision." You'd have to agree with Helen Keller. At 91, J.C. Penny was asked how his eyesight was. He replied that his sight was failing but his vision had never been better.

Isn't that great? Think about it! When your vision is clear it becomes easy to make decisions. When a person has no vision of a better way of life, they automatically shut themselves in a prison. They limit themselves to a life without hope. This frequently happens when a person has seriously tried on a number of occasions to win only to meet with failure time after time. Repeated failures can damage a person's self-image and cause them to lose sight of their potential. They, therefore, make a Decision to give up and resign themselves to their fate.

Take the first step in predicting your own prosperous future. Build a mental picture of exactly how you would like to live. Make a firm Decision to hold onto that vision and positive ways to improve everything will begin to flow into your mind. Many people make a beautiful vision of how they would like to live or what they would like from their business but because they cannot see how they're going to make it all happen they let the vision go. If they knew how they were going to make it happen or get it they would have a plan, not a vision. There's no inspiration in a plan but there sure is in a vision.

When you get the vision freeze-frame it in your mind with a Decision and don't worry about how you're going to do it or where the resources will come from. Charge your Decision with enthusiasm. That's important. Refuse to worry about how it will happen. There is a power much greater than you that never expresses itself other than perfectly and that perfection will take care of that responsibility. There is no situation that isn't made worse by worry. Worry never solves anything. Worry never prevents anything. Worry never heals anything. Worry serves only one purpose; it makes matters worse. James Kurtz said, "If we worry, we don't trust. If we trust, we don't worry. Worry does not empty tomorrow of its grief, but it does empty today of its joy." Worry seems to be a national pastime but it's also a sad waste of time. Remember what Dr. Kurtz said, "Worry empties today of its joy."

Don't worry. Be happy. Have faith. Worrying about lack is a clear indication there is a serious misunderstanding with respect to our source of supply. By our source, I mean you and me. We are both receiving every good that comes Into our life from the same source. There is only one source of supply and that is Spirit. Everything comes from Spirit. When you clearly understand that you will find making a Decision is something much easier to do. Every Decision you make is based on one of two points. One, you're going to gain a profit or two, you're going to avoid a loss. Most people who work for a corporation believe their pay comes from the company. When I am conducting a seminar, I make it very clear their pay comes from Spirit. Their only source of supply. It merely comes through their company.

When you truly understand the source of your supply and then enhance your understanding with the laws by which Spirit works you will be able to make a Decision and hold the picture of the successful outcome as a result of that Decision. Knowing that Spirit will instantly begin sending to you whatever you require for the manifestation of your picture.

I am well aware that there are millions of people who will laugh at you if you attempted to get them to accept what I've just said. However, it is important for you to remember that those same people are not able to explain why they are rejecting it or why it cannot happen. Our company has a great program called Born Rich. This Born Rich program explains why it will happen. We've come up with another program that's incredible it'll show anyone how to earn a six or seven-figure income. It is called Disciplined Income Acceleration and it deals with the unlimited supply of money. The DIA program will show anyone as I've just mentioned how to earn a six or a seven-figure income.

However, this brings us right back to the start. Earning that amount of money requires a Decision. One of the instructors in the disciplined income acceleration program, Jerry Robert, wrote a marvelous book, "Conquering Life's Obstacles." I found an interesting idea and one that you can gain tremendous benefit from in your efforts to become a more effective decision-maker. Listen to this. "Advanced decision making." Isn't that great? Think about it. We make advanced bookings when we fly somewhere, that's quite common. We make advanced reservations to eliminate any confusion or problems when the time arrives for the journey. We do the same with renting a car for the same reason.

Think of the problems you will eliminate by making many of the decisions you must make well in advance. I'll give you an excellent example. As I am preparing this message it is Ramadan in Malaysia. A time when all practicing Muslims fast. I was in an office yesterday in Kuala Lumpur and I was asked if I would like a cup of tea or coffee. I replied that I would, and I appreciated a cup of tea. the lady next to me was then asked if she would like a cup and she replied, "No I'm fasting." I smiled and said that was an advanced Decision this lady had made. When she was asked, she did not have to decide whether she wanted anything or not. Whether she was thirsty or not was not a consideration. A Decision had previously been made and her advanced Decision was well tempered with discipline. (Michele and Bob have a great program to assist with diet called, Be Your Perfect Weight. It includes the affirmation song I Am Now At My Perfect Weight.)

The exact same concept works with a person when they are on a diet. To lose weight their decisions are made in advance. If they are offered a slice of chocolate cake or some Bavarian cream pie they don't have to say, "Gee that looks good. I wonder if I should." The Decision is made in advance. You might want to read Jerry Robert's book. It's an excellent article on advanced decision-making.

I made a Decision a long time ago that I would not participate in discussions of why something cannot be done. The only compensation you will ever receive for participating in or giving energy to that type of discussion is something you do not want. I always find it amazing at the number of seemingly intelligent people who persist in dragging you into these negative brainstorming sessions. In one breath these people tell you they seriously want to accomplish a particular objective and in the next breath, they begin talking about why they can't. Think of how much more of life they would enjoy by making a Decision that they will no longer participate in that type of negative energy.

Permit me to caution you. Advanced decisions must be mixed with an ample supply of discipline. All peak performers understand and use discipline. The program I previously referred to that my company conducts where we teach people how to earn a six and a seven-figure income is called Disciplined Income Acceleration. Discipline is to success what carbon is to steel. Any Decision you make must be backed by discipline. Research indicates that highly successful individuals make decisions very quickly and change those decisions very slowly if and when they are changed at all. By comparison, the person who rarely enjoys any degree of success makes decisions very slowly and they change their decisions very quickly and often. Those individuals who rarely win generally have the habit of being influenced in their decision-making by the opinions of others. While their successful counterparts follow their own counsel.

The most natural thing in the world for you to do in life is probably the most destructive insofar as succeeding at anything is concerned. That is following the crowd. Historically the crowd has always been traveling in the wrong direction. You were encouraged to be like the other kids when you were young. You have been conditioned to follow the crowd. In many schools, you were even dressed like the other kids. Well, you're not a child any longer and you're not like the other kids. You are unique. That is what makes the Mona Lisa so valuable. There is only one and similarly, there is only one of you. Be yourself. Breakaway from the crowd. Make your own decisions.

The humanistic psychologist Dr. Abraham Maslow, who devoted his life to studying self-actualized people, stated very clearly that we should follow our inner guide and not be swayed by the opinions of others or outside circumstances. Maslow's research showed that the decision-makers in life had a number of things in common, most importantly they did work they felt was worthwhile and important. They found work a pleasure and there was little distinction between work and play. Dr. Maslow said, "To be self-actualized you must not only be doing work you consider to be important, you must do it well and enjoy it." Dr. Maslow recorded that these super performers, these superior performers, had values, those qualities in their personalities they considered to be worthwhile and important. Their values were not imposed by society, parents, or other people in their lives. They made their own decisions. Like their work, they chose and developed their values themselves.

Your life is important and, at its best, life is short. You have the potential to do anything you choose and do it well, but you must make decisions. And when the time for a Decision arrives you must make your Decision where you are with what you've got.

Let me leave you with the words of two great decision-makers, William James and Thomas Edison. William James suggested that "compared to what we ought to be... we are making use of only a small part of our physical and mental resources. Stating this concept broadly, the human individual thus lives far within his limits. He possesses powers of various sorts which he habitually fails to use." Years later Thomas Edison said, and I quote, "If we all did the things, we are capable of doing we would literally astound ourselves."

By making a simple Decision the greatest minds of the past are available to you. You can literally learn how to turn your wildest dreams into reality. Decide. Decide to study the lives of the great leaders of the past and couple that Decision with the Decision to develop all of that potential that William James and Thomas Edison were referring to. You have it, use it. Put this valuable information to use. Recognize the greatness which exists within you. You have limitless powers of potential and ability waiting to be developed. Start today. There's never any time that's better than the present. Be all that you're capable of being. Listen carefully to our star of affirmations, Michele, as she gets your right brain involved in a left-brain activity. Listen to the decision song again and again.

Decision
Decision Decision Decision

Winners make decisions fast
Losers make them slow
Winning is a choice just decide and go

Decision
Decision Decision Decision

Make Decisions be decisive
Show the world you're bold
You'll be loved you'll be admired
You'll attract your share of gold

Decision
Decision Decision Decision

It's a single mental move that
turns the dark to Light
So make Decisions be decisive
Your fears will take flight

Decision
Decision Decision Decision

Winning is a blast
winners make decisions fast
make decisions
Come on everybody
You're a winner yes you are
Come on now you can do it

Success

Success. How about that. Imagine that it is tomorrow morning and you're just waking up. You find at the foot of your bed beautifully wrapped in gold foil a package with your name on it. You spring to your feet grab the gift and tear it open. Inside you find success. Success for the rest of your life, it's yours, you've got it! Some kind guide left it while you slept.

Let me ask you, what would your new gift look like? What color would it be? How big was the package it arrived in? How would you describe it to the next person you spoke with on the telephone? How did it make you feel receiving a gift like that? Would you be excited knowing that you had in your hot, little hands success for the rest of your life? You're very likely smiling at this point and possibly thinking this guy, Proctor, should be writing comic books. This is a great fantasy.

Listen up, my friend. This is no fantasy. The important points I just spoke about, the part that said you had the gift of success for the rest of your life, is a fact. You've got it. You may not know that you have it. In other words, you might not recognize this wonderful truth and if you don't you certainly have not been able to enjoy or share your success with your loved ones. But you've got it.

Look at it this way. Bring your full conscious attention to bear on my voice, the sound of my voice, how I am sounding out each word. Next, shift your attention to an object that is within your site. I can see a white, cordless telephone in front of me. Bring your attention to bear on an object, any object in front of you. If you're listening to this in your automobile focus on your rearview mirror. All right now, I want you to think of the ease with which you flip your attention from the sound of my voice to whatever object you chose to focus on. It took no effort. Well, with the same amount of effort you can literally go from being unsuccessful to successful. From feelings of lack and limitation to a feeling of abundance in all areas of your life.

Listen.
TheMysticalExperience.com/NPSongs

That's it. Success is a direction that you choose. It has nothing to do with how much money you have, how old you are, where you are, who you are, or what you've done in the past, or even what you are presently doing at this specific moment. It's the direction you are going. It's the direction you choose to go with your life, and it is your choice.

Activate your imagination for a moment. We're going to create a hypothetical situation of an individual who is filing for bankruptcy, going through divorce court, on crutches, with no particular place to sleep tonight, nothing to eat, yet the individual is successful.

The old conditioning or the old paradigm you might be operating with could be causing you to think a person in the situation I just described, bankruptcy and all, sure doesn't look or sound successful. And, of course, that is generally where the problem with most people begins. They're going by what they see and hear. Which is pretty natural. That is what we're taught to do from birth. That kind of thinking will cripple you every time. Mentally focusing on present physical results will only give you more of the same type of physical results.

This hypothetical individual who was surrounded by the overwhelming negative results could have suddenly become aware of the bold, bare, beautiful truth that success is a direction which begins with a decision and has absolutely nothing to do with anything outside of himself. At the precise moment, the hypothetical individual made a decision about what he wanted, and he knew what he wanted, and then made another critical decision, he would let go of the past and move in the direction of his dream. That's it. That was the magic moment that made him successful.

Success is achieved by making a decision. Earl Nightingale used to tell a story of a successful businessman who was asked when he became successful. He replied, "I became successful when I was sleeping on a park bench because I knew where I was going, and I knew that I would get there." the obvious question then is if success is that simple why do so few people participate? They don't know and they don't know that they don't know. That is why so few people enjoy success.

If you had a couple of tons of gold bullion buried in your backyard but you didn't know it was there how much good would it do you? It wouldn't do you any good because you didn't know it was there. The only real problem anyone will ever have is ignorance. Not knowing. There are so few people who are truly successful and so many others who desperately work hard all of their lives attempting to be successful, that the average person is diluted by an overwhelming amount of evidence which indicates success is hard to obtain. And those who do achieve success are either lucky or extremely brilliant. The great majority of the population is so busy attempting to make ends meet that they never take the time to actually do proper research or make an in-depth study of highly successful people.

Every person who has made such a study has arrived at the same shocking conclusion. Success is merely a decision. That's it. You must decide what you want and then begin moving toward it. You decide, now, right where you are, and you begin with whatever you've got. That's it. Don't argue with it. Success, as a word or as a concept, has fascinated people for centuries. It has probably been analyzed and discussed as often, if not more than any other word in this or any language. However, relative to the total population of any country there are only a few people anywhere who understand what success is all about. What the word means. Although there would understandably be some, there are very few people alive who have invested more time studying this word than myself.

I have spent almost all day every day for 33 years analyzing success. Over the years I have had many failures, but I've also had numerous, exciting wins. I've enjoyed these experiences on many continents around the world. I believe it is important for you to understand this did not all take place in my own backyard and there have been millions of dollars involved. The wins and the failures have both proven to be extraordinary, personal learning experiences. I share this with you in support of my claim to understand the subject success. I have come to the firm conclusion that the very finest and most accurate definition of success I can give you is one my former employer and associate, the late Earl Nightingale, gave to me many years ago. "Success is the progressive realization of a worthy ideal."

When you give this definition of success the thought, I have given it and tested it as I have, you will realize just how perfect a definition it is. Earl Nightingale invested 17 and one-half years searching for this secret, this definition before he found it. He left this world four years later without changing one word. Add to that, what I previously mentioned, that I accepted Earl Nightingale's definition of success and have worked with it for well over 30 years, and you'll not alter a single word. Success is the progressive realization of a worthy ideal.

I'm really making this sound simple, aren't I? Well, it certainly appears simple. But like so many other things in life that appear fairly simple they're not that easy, nor are they that simple. They require thought. Think of it this way. Intellectually most everyone would think they understood Earl Nightingale's definition of success. "The progressive realization of a worthy ideal." Just decide what you want. Go for it. But there's more to it than that. You have to take it apart and analyze it.

Let's take that word 'progressive'. Progressive does not mean that you would go at it with everything you've got for a day or two and then slack off for a week until someone comes along to wind your stem and cause you to take another run at it. Progressive, in my dictionary, is defined a few different ways but one of the definitions says this, "increasing in severity, proceeding in intensity."

I believe that's what Earl Nightingale had in mind. The 'realization' part indicates an ever-increasing awareness. Which would indicate that the materialization of the 'worthy ideal' is becoming more obvious. Then the 'worthy ideal' becomes very interesting.

Let's take 'ideal'. First, James Allen, the great Victorian author, put it so well when he suggested that an ideal is an idea that we have fallen in love with. Meaning that it consumes our intellectual self, our emotional self, and our physical self. I like that.

Now, for the 'worthy' segment of this magnificent definition of success. The word 'worthy' is the stumbling block for most people. Misunderstanding this part keeps the masses in the foothills, wandering aimlessly, frequently frustrated, often angry. And too often miserably disappointed with themselves and their accomplishments. It's like the little boy said to his dad, "Okay, dad. We got the big house, the two-car garage, the cars, the boat, and the place by the lake. What's next?" most people are trying to shore up their self-image to the point where they feel worthy of the good that they desire.

Consider this. You are the highest form of creation on the face of the earth. You are worthy of whatever good you desire. The question you should be asking then is, "is my idea worthy of me? Is it worthy of my attention, my interest? Should I be giving or trading my life for this idea? Is it worthy of my love?"

When you begin to look at Earl Nightingale's definition, from that point of view everything changes. What you want becomes so very important. Unfortunately, there are only about one or two people out of every hundred who recognize what they truly want. Think about it. Only a couple out of every hundred grabs the brass ring. I have come to the conclusion that the vast majority of the population rejects the real want every time it floats to the surface of their consciousness. Their self-image will not accept it. Or they are afraid that if they even mention it to anyone that they'd be laughed at. So, they immediately begin to think of the reasons why they could not possibly have it.

Bad programming, negative surroundings, and the lack of proper information and support keep most people lost in the foothills. They never enjoy the view from the top of the mountain. Because we are inundated with information on goals and the fact that you must have them to win, we find a few people setting them. However, these goals are typically for cars, money, or buildings. All of these things are nice, and we should have and enjoy them. Well, let us clearly understand. They would rarely, if ever, represent a worthy ideal. They are merely substitutions for worthy ideals which is probably why we call them goals. How could a person become consumed with the idea of buying a car or a building when we know we can own a fleet of cars without much trouble.

I know one man who has personally bought 500 houses. These things would have a difficult time qualifying as worthy ideals. They're a collection of things. Please, do not get me wrong. I enjoy nice cars and houses but there's no way I'll trade my life for them. You must be wondering at this point, "What does Proctor want?" Well, I'll tell you what I want. I want to build a global organization dedicated to improving the quality of life worldwide. To create products and services with like-minded people who have a common purpose. To live and work in a prosperous environment that encourages productivity so that we may improve the service we render to our family, our company, our community. And ultimately our nation. That is what I want and I'm progressively realizing it. Because my worthy ideal is so big and powerful it has attracted wonderful people to me from all around the world. I never doubt if I can do it. I am doing it. And I will be doing it for the rest of my life here on this planet.

Other wonderful people have bought into my dream. They have said, "that's what I want too. Let's do it together." that's the kind of want that is worthy of you. When you are progressively realizing that type of a worthy ideal, you're a definite success. I could spoil your week if I told you about some of the terrible things that I've attracted to me in pursuit of my dream, but I've never wavered. Successful people never do. The truth of the matter is that everything which has happened has strengthened me. And just like nature, when a hurricane hits all the weak structures and deadwood gets blown away that's the same in life. Don't be disappointed when other people let you down or betray you. Keep going. Nature abhors a vacuum. A stronger form of support is on the way and nature's creating a space for them.

Let's take a close look at you, your real nature, and then the idea of success. The very core of your being is spiritual. The essence of God is the very nucleus of you. You are a spiritual being.

You have an intellect, and you live in a physical body. Now stay with me here. Spirit is always for expansion and fuller expression. It is never for disintegration. God, Spirit, operates in an orderly manner which is perfect. We refer to this perfect action as law. This is frequently referred to as the laws of the universe. Spirit expresses itself through you. You are an instrument of God.

When you are working in harmony with God or Spirit you are working with an infinite source of supply. As an instrument, the only limits placed on you are the limits that you place on yourself. Because your basic nature is infinite, in truth, there is no limit to what you are capable of.

As a people when we permitted ourselves the luxury of holding the image or the want of traveling in an automobile rather than a horse and carriage, we built one, when we then afforded ourselves the luxury of having the image or the want of air travel, we did it. We introduced ourselves to another kingdom. We flew higher than the birds. It has been the same with the facts, the phone, the television, ordinary people's extraordinary wants, and bingo. Accomplishments.

What do you really want? Recognize it. Admit it. Holler it from the treetops. "This is what I really want." You see, my want is real, it's happening.

"Born Rich" the freeing philosophy which is the foundation of my life's work is now available in Chinese, French, Portuguese, English, and it's going around the world from North America, to Asia, to South America. Your spiritual core keeps jabbing at your consciousness. Be quiet and listen.

What do you really want? Everyone wants something big, real big. Don't deny it or reject it. Grab it, write it on paper. You don't have to know how it will happen; you only have to know it will happen. God had big plans for you when you were created. That's why you were given such awesome potential. The most erudite scientist alive today will not even guess at what you are capable of. Since God had such big plans for you wouldn't it make good sense for you to have big plans for you? What do you really want? The picture of greatness keeps popping up in your mind. Everyone wants to be great at something, that's our nature. Know that.

You would not even be able to mentally see yourself doing something if you couldn't do it. I like what Stella Terrill Mann said, "If you can hold it in your head, you can hold it in your hand."

What do you want? So, what if it's still a fantasy. That's how the train and the plane and the car and the facts began. Fantasize. Play with the beautiful images, then nail one. Say, "That's it. That's what I want. That is worthy of me. I'll wake up every morning and be excited about trading my life for that. Yes, I really will."

If your friends, relatives, and neighbors laugh at you get away from them. Don't you dare let them pull you down. There are others who will pretend to be your friends, who go around moody and playing, "Poor me." get away from them. They'll rob you of your dream. You don't have to get better, you're already beautiful. God didn't make any rejects. The progressive realization of what you want will bring with it a greater awareness. Your power and magnetism will compound. Your want must be big, beautiful, and you must really want it.

It does not matter if anyone else wants it or if they want you to want it. It only matters that you want it. If you truly want to live a successful life you must be progressively realizing a worthy ideal. That is success. And that does require change. You're going to meet up with resistance but by following the suggestions on this program and the suggestions on persistence section you will understand that you must choose a big powerful ideal. I'm going to call it the want of your life. Understand the resistance will be strong, it will. But by properly preparing for this resistance, you'll beat it. You will win.

Keep in mind that the degree of resistance you will encounter is in direct ratio to the size and the nature of the idea with which you begin to work. The visionaries have always been persecuted before they were recognized and rewarded, but that's okay. They understood what was happening. They realized that when people don't understand something they have a tendency to ridicule and criticize it. I've taken a piece of literature on resistance by William Penn Patrick that I truly enjoy reading. It helps me and I know it's going to help you. Prepare your mind for what Penn Patrick said. Be quiet and enjoy it, learn.

He said, "No person, ideal, or institution becomes great until Great Resistance has been encountered. Greatness cannot be achieved until this concept is understood.

Unfortunately, the average person is ignorant of this rule to achievement. Mr. and Miss Average, in their ignorance, are fearful and reluctant to encounter even slight resistance. They don't want to make waves or be criticized, and they incorrectly feel that criticism will hold them back and prevent their happiness from being realized. In truth, the opposite is the case.

Take note: when we begin to change we are first given resistance by our loved ones, for they fear change because change means facing the unknown. When we begin to make rapid progress or commitment to rapid progress, we have roadblocks thrown up by our friends and relatives. They begin to resist by negative comments and actions which are devices to cause you to maintain the status quo.

Now, if you are to achieve great progress, you must prevail against those closest to you. This is difficult and requires courage because you desire to please and not hurt those you love. The truth is that great harm befalls your loved ones when you fail to be yourself, to do your thing, and become what you are meant to become. This is so because you lose your enthusiasm for life. Your growth process stops, and your self-esteem diminishes. Those negatives are reversed when you stand your ground. And when you have prevailed your loved ones gain a new and higher respect for you. History records countless events which prove the point.

We are fortunate to have such great resistance. This resistance is evidence of our greatness, and it provides us with the energy to prevail, to conquer, and to dominate. These next few short years will record a brilliant history and establish a permanent place for our way of life – which is Freedom to be and to work out our dreams for a great world, for ourselves, for children, and all of mankind.

Understand our battle and be glorified that you are a part of the making of history. The work you do today will provide new freedom and hope for millions yet to come. Stand tall in the face of our enemy. Your resolution and commitment will seize his heart with fear, and he will fade into oblivion. And that is the law of life."

All right, my friend, that's it. Now you understand what must be done. Hopefully, you are acutely aware of the point I stressed and the message we recorded for you on persistence. Success and Persistence do go together like the chicken and the egg. You will not have one without the other. You will not persist if the want is not the right want for you. And if you don't persist you will not be successful. You want success, I know you do. Go back to the foot of your bed and open that imaginary gift. Make the decision, accept your gift from God. Success for the rest of your life, it's yours. Come and climb the mountains with us. We'll enjoy your company. "Success is the progressive realization of a worthy ideal."

Communication

TheMysticalExperience.com/NPSongs

All right. The whole universe is related, and we are all in the same family. Can Michele ever sing. On this topic I want to talk to you about how our thought energy affects other people.

Hello, this is Bob Proctor, and this message is on Communication. Effective Communication is absolutely essential if you want to enjoy a truly successful life. You cannot function in a truly dynamic manner for any prolonged period of time by yourself. You require other people. There are thousands of tracks I could run on preparing this message for you on the subject of Communication. Communication covers such a broad spectrum: television, the fax, the phone. We could literally focus on thousands of different directions.

I want to focus on a very narrow but important area of Communication. The concept this message deals with is either not understood or ignored by most people. I'm going to suggest that few people know what I'm going to talk about. Most of us are conditioned to be very self-serving and we must reverse that concept and build a new paradigm. If you're going to make winning a conditioned part of your nature you must make helping other people automatic in your life.

To be truly effective in speaking a language you must think in that language. A person who is fluently bilingual thinks in both languages. They're not mentally translating every word they hear from one language to another. Winners automatically think of helping other people. Now, since you think in pictures or images the purpose of this message is to assist you in becoming more effective at transmitting images to other people. Images that will help them. Look at it this way, in his philosophy on success Napoleon Hill said and I quote, "I will induce others to serve me because of my willingness to serve others."

That is a nice idea. There are some people who will tell you that's an old-fashioned idea, and they are correct. It is much older than either of us. The truth is that the idea has always been here. It is like the lyrics in a very famous song that suggests love was here before the stars, and of course, it was, and so was the law behind Napoleon Hill's suggestion that he would induce others to serve him because of his willingness to serve others. That's just another way of phrasing the law of cause and effect, sowing and reaping, action-reaction.

In almost every seminar I conduct I make mention of the fact that money is a reward we receive for the service that we render. The beautiful truth is that everything that we receive in our life is a reward for service that we render. You can improve the quantity and the quality of rewards by improving your service. Keep that concept fresh in your mind. In fact, fix it in your subconscious mind. And you could do that by repeatedly listening to this recorded message and reading this chapter again. When that idea is fixed in your subconscious mind you will never have to concern yourself with receiving ever again. Helping others will become automatic. You'll be locked on and locked into the universally rewarding activity of giving. How's that for a beginning? Do you like the track that I have chosen to run on? I'm sure you do.

Now, to move you into a more receptive vibration to help you become a little more subjective I am going to ask you to listen to Michele sing Communication again. As you listen, bring every speck of conscious attention that you can muster to the lyrics of her song. These lyrics have been written especially for this communication message. There is a deep meaning buried in this song and as you listen it is important to remember that everything is energy, and thought is energy. And you can think, I can think, we can connect, we're related, yes, we really are.

Communication Song Lyrics

The Universe is related
We're all in the same family
Vibration makes nature a part of you
And you with nature a part of me

Races must come together before it gets too late
Let's understand we're really one
And begin to communicate
Races must come together with love to replace hate
Let's understand we're really one
And begin to communicate

As we study the law vibration
We'll view other people from our heart
The whole world will be one nation
And communication will be an art
Straight from our heart

Races must come together before it gets too late
Let's understand we're really one
And begin to communicate
Yes races must come together with love to replace hate
Let's understand we're really one
And begin to communicate
Let's begin to communicate

So be quiet my love and listen
From within you will feel a sound
The Creator's voice is telling us
Air's made from the same stuff as the ground

Yes, the Creator's voice has spoken
Air is made from the same stuff as the ground
As the ground

Do you spend much time thinking of how you are related to the universe? If you're like most people, you very likely do not. You're probably busy doing whatever you do. Because of the type of work, I have chosen, I think of my relationship with the universe often, every day. In fact, it's how I spend my days. The truth of how we're related becomes more interesting and more obvious to me every day. It may be to you as well. If it hasn't, I'm sure as you invest more time and energy in this direction, you'll discover the same truths.

There are certain aspects of this relationship you'll have to consider if you're going to enjoy the benefits of Communication or the Communication concept that I'm going to share with you. I want you to think about the lyrics from the last verse of Michele's song. "So be quiet my love and listen, from within you will feel a sound. The creator's voice is telling us air is made from the same stuff as the ground."

Now think about this. "So be quiet my love and listen." To be quiet you must relax your mind/body. Shut down your physical senses. Get in touch with your own feelings. "From within you will feel a sound. The creator's voice is telling us..." All right now, listen closely to this beautiful truth. The sound of God evolves around the law of vibration, and on a conscious level vibrations are referred to as feelings. By shutting down your senses and blocking out all outside distractions and being quiet you will feel a sound. And get this, the air is made from the same stuff as the ground. Air is energy. The earth is energy. Everything is energy. Thought is energy.

In fact, thought is one of the most potent of all forms of energy. It's on one of the highest frequencies. Through recorded history theology has constantly reminded us that everything is the expression of one power. Air is made from the same stuff as the ground and so are you. More recently science has proven that everything is the expression of one power. Both science and theology have cautioned us time and time again that the entire universe operates by exact law. One of the laws is the law of vibration. Do you remember the lyrics from that verse?

As we study the law of vibration
We'll view other people from our heart

The whole world will be one nation
And communication will be an art
Straight from our heart

Isn't that beautiful? I want to refer now to the law of vibration. To do this I'm going to ask you to go to page 110 in my book 'You Were Born Rich.' What I wrote there is very relevant to this particular message on Communication. On page 110 it says the law of vibration accounts for the difference between mind and matter. You could say between the air and the earth. Between the physical and the non-physical worlds. According to the law of vibration, we postulate that everything vibrates or moves. Nothing rests, nothing is idle. Everything is in a constant state of motion and therefore there is no such thing as inertia or state of rest. From the most ethereal to the most gross form of matter, everything is in a constant state of vibration. Moving from the lowest to the highest degree of vibration we discover there are literally millions upon millions of intervening levels, or degrees, from the electron to the universe. Everything is in vibratory motion. Energy is manifested in all varying degrees of vibration. Rates of vibration are called frequencies and the higher the frequency the more potent the force. Since thought is one of the highest forms of vibration it is very potent in nature and therefore it must be understood by everyone.

Now, the law of vibration may be explained in many different ways depending upon the purpose for which it is being explained. In this chapter, however, it is our intention to confine our inquiry to thoughts alone. Now I want you to think about this, all right? Now come with me as we leave the law of vibration for a few moments and we'll both focus our conscious attention on you and your world. I'm working with the premise that you want to cause a mega improvement in your results. To make any improvement you must improve yourself and you can do that by becoming a more effective communicator. Since you live simultaneously on three different planes of life it would necessarily follow that you communicate on all three planes simultaneously. You live in a physical body, you have an intellect, and you are a perfect spiritual expression. You could say that the giant part of you is much like an iceberg. It is not visible to the human eye which would indicate that much of our communications are on that non-physical, non-intellectual level. That is where vibration will come back into this message.

The super communicators understand how to send and receive messages very effectively on all three levels. These people are always working with the law of vibration. They clearly understand that through vibration everything is connected. The only difference between one thing and another is the density, or amplitude, of vibration. It's as I explained from 'You Were Born Rich.' Vibration explains the difference between mind and matter. You will recall the various levels of vibration are referred to as frequencies. There are millions of frequencies, each one having one above and one below, all of them connected. There is no line of demarcation.

Frequencies come together like the colors of a rainbow. You're not able to tell where one starts and the other stops because they are all together. Now think of this. Your brain, every cell in your brain, operates on a frequency. Every person is the same. You have a mental dial in your marvelous mind which enables you to tune in on the other person's frequency. It is well to remember that the other person has exactly the same ability. I rarely pay attention to what a person is saying relative to what I feel. I'm much more interested in the vibrations I am receiving. By playing this message over and over and over again, by learning the lyrics to the song, and then singing along with Michele, you'll find yourself becoming more aware of what you are feeling. You'll become more sensitive to the vibrations around you.

I've been working with this every day for over 30 years, so my sensitivity switch has a hair-trigger. If I'm around, you, I will tune in very quickly. Believe me, this is worth serious consideration. If you merely begin humming Michele's tune, you'll trigger these ideas to come into your consciousness, and through repetition, you'll definitely heighten your awareness and you'll begin to communicate on a higher dimension. One that is much more effective and most certainly more accurate and dependable. You'll become sensitive to the thousands of messages that are flying around every day. Messages which you very likely have been missing in the past.

This will assist you in becoming much more effective at transmitting images to other people that will help them. Images that will make them feel good about themselves. When you do this, you'll be following some excellent advice that Lord Chesterfield gave to his son when he said, "My son, cause other people to like themself just a little bit better, and I'll promise you this, they will like you very much."

That's exactly where this form of effective Communication begins. Listen to what Webster had to say about effective communications. I quote, "Effective; in a condition to produce desired results, efficient, powerful." And on communications, he said, "An information means of passing from one place to another, a connecting passage." With that information if we were to redefine our objective you could say you want to build a connecting passage between your mind and the mind of another individual, or group of individuals so that you can transmit images from your mind to theirs, and from their mind to yours in a more efficient, powerful manner.

We are motivated by images. When you get a beautiful picture on the screen of your mind, a smile, a happy look comes on your face. You feel good inside. Your behavior improves. This is an important point. We invented the word feeling to express our conscious awareness of vibrations. Good feelings, positive vibrations. Bad feelings, negative vibrations. Positive images on the screen of your mind cause your body to move into a healthy vibration. Remember, your body holds massive energy and at high speed of vibration. Your thoughts set up new vibrations.

All right now, listen carefully and do as I suggest. Visualize yourself in the ballroom of a large hotel. At the front of the room, there's a very large, white screen. You are about to project movies or slides onto this screen. The ballroom is filled with people. There are about seven or eight hundred people seated there, chatting away to each other. In a projection booth high at the back of the room there's a 35-millimeter projector filled with slides. The slides are of the wonders of the world.

The lights in the ballroom begin to dim, the chatter fades, and as Goldsmith said, "The thunder of silence fills the room." In your hand is a remote control switch for the 35-millimeter projector. With your thumb, you touch a button. An order that is not visible to your eye is instantly and silently fired off to the projector, and bingo, a slide drops in front of the light and is projected onto the large screen in the front of the room. All seven or eight hundred people who are seated in that ballroom are now looking at a beautiful, colored picture of the Taj Mahal. Your thumb touches the button again and now everyone is looking at millions of tons of water rushing over the falls at Niagara. The entire screen is illuminated with an exciting, nighttime, color picture of Niagara Falls.

My friend, there is no ballroom, no projector, no audience, no Taj Mahal or Niagara. Only words that I recorded which are now vibrations, light messages, are being sent from your recorder to your brain. They are picked up by your hearing sense. This light message, or vibration, is traveling at a ridiculous speed down the nerve passageway in your body and striking a group of cells in your brain. Cells that are already vibrating because the law of vibration decrees that nothing rests.

You'll remember I read that from 'You Were Born Rich.' when this particular group of cells is affected by the sound of my voice they instantly increase in the amplitude of vibration. And the images which were there in the cells in your brain fly on the screen of your mind. The images of the Taj Mahal and Niagara Falls were quietly resting in the cells of your brain. My words activated them. Images of the ballroom, the projector, and the seven or eight hundred people were all in cells in your brain. Even the button that you touched with your thumb, the image of it was in your brain as well.

Have you any idea how many pictures are tucked away in your brain? I doubt if you could count that high. There are happy and sad pictures, pictures that will depress or excite us, pictures that will speed us up or slow us down, pictures that will make us feel wonderful. The words you use, the words you choose to direct at the next person you meet will very likely determine the images that fly onto the screen of their marvelous mind, and that determines their vibration.

I have already brought to your attention that we live on different levels on the intellectual level. We communicate through words, gestures, and writing. Pay close attention to what I am about to do right now. I will use words that will cause images to register in your mind's eye. These images will show you how gestures are used to communicate.

Visualize an elderly woman kneeling on one knee with her arms openly outstretched. A small, two-year-old child is running towards her. They both have broad smiles on their faces. Those arms are waiting to be wrapped around that small child. Outstretched arms are a gesture of love. They are saying, "come to me. You are welcome. I want to hug you." Words are not required. The child will get the message.

And, of course, on an intellectual level, we also communicate through writing. A book is a picture painted with words. A good author will create a movie in their mind and then choose the words that will hopefully activate in your mind the same picture they see in their mind. You have very likely read a book and then gone to a movie that was based on the book. Odds are you were disappointed in the movie. You were disappointed because the movie you created in your mind while reading the book was much better than the one that you viewed at the theater. You must understand, however, your imagination did not have any of the restrictions or constraints the movie maker was faced with. That's worth remembering. Your imagination has no limits. Which is why Albert Einstein said, "The imagination is more important than knowledge."

Through the aid of your imagination, you can see and hear yourself communicating in a much more effective manner with the next person you meet. You can do that right now even though you may be alone. Mentally you can hear the words that you will carefully choose. You can mentally see the gestures that you will use. The benefits of effective Communication are certainly worthy of a respectable amount of practice.

Let's take a moment right now and review. On an intellectual level, you communicate with words, gestures, and writing. The brain is where we believe the intellect to be resident. Begin to associate and view in your mind your words, gestures, and writing as light messages, vibrations that are directed at the other person's brain. These vibrations will activate pictures in the other person's mind. Make certain your words, gestures, and writing trigger positive pictures. This is why salespeople are taught to sell benefits. Sell the sizzle and not the steak.

Elmer Wheeler said, "People don't buy quarter-inch drills because they want quarter-inch drills. They buy quarter-inch drills because they want quarter-inch holes." Remember, benefits, benefits, benefits. Make the other person feel good. Create pictures in your mind of the other person enjoying more of life. Send that kind of an Image to the other person. The universe will send back every speck of good. This is where the law vibration re-enters the picture.

As we study the law of vibration, we will view other people from our heart. The early Greeks referred to the universal subconscious mind, the emotional mind as the heart. That part of the mind which connects you or me to everyone and everything. You communicate heart to heart through vibration, more commonly referred to as feelings. Make a mental note of what I am about to say. My teacher, Val Vandewall explained this to me many years ago and it is one of the most powerful truths I have ever learned. "Words are noise. Vibration never lies." Let me repeat that. "Words are noise. Vibration never lies."

The seat of your emotions seems to rest in the solar plexus. That is where you pick up vibrations. You frequently refer to this as a gut feeling. When you see a tragedy, you often say it made you feel sick to your stomach. When you fall in love where do you get that good feeling? Now, let's switch gears for a moment. How many times have you sensed something was troubling a loved one and you asked them what's wrong and they replied nothing? You knew they were not being honest with you. Something was wrong. You knew it because you felt it. Your ears heard their words, "nothing," but heart to heart you also picked up what they were transmitting. Vibrations never lie.

Intellectually they are saying one thing and emotionally they are saying the opposite. That is commonly referred to in psychiatric circles as a double-binding message. And double binding messages never produce desired results. If you want to communicate effectively you must mean what you say and say what you mean. It is not difficult to be saying one thing and thinking or being emotionally involved with something else. Understand that while your words are activating a set of positive pictures in a person's mind your vibrations could easily be activating the opposite. When that happens the other person's mind is in a confused state and not capable of any intelligent action. They'll feel confused and probably not know why.

Think of the number of salespeople who are telling their prospects they want to help them and at the same time they are thinking of the commissions they are hoping to earn from the sale. These salespeople are the same ones whose income remains in the danger zone. When the salespeople who earn six and seven-figure incomes absolutely love what they do, that love is being transmitted to those that they meet. They love helping other people benefit from the product or service that they render.

Look at the great entertainers. They love sharing their talent with an appreciative audience, an audience that is receiving what they want. The positive energy moves back and forth always expanding. That is synergy and synergy is hot energy. The same law that applies and is used by the professional entertainer applies to you and me. When we are communicating what we want to do is find out what the other person wants and give it to them. And remember you must mean what you say and say what you mean. When your thoughts, words, gestures, and feelings are in sync with the other person that is synergism. And remember synergy is hot energy.

Now, before we leave, I want to hit on some of the salient points from this message. Listen carefully. The purpose of this message was to assist you in becoming more effective at transmitting images to the other person that would help them. Effective communication is essential to enjoy a truly successful life. You cannot function in a truly dynamic manner by yourself for any prolonged period of time. You need other people. To make winning a part of your conditioned nature you must make helping other people automatic in your life. You can induce others to serve you through your willingness to serve others. Everything you receive in life is a reward you receive for serving others. You will improve the quantity and the quality of your rewards by improving your service.

Everything in the universe is related. Everything is energy. Thought is energy. You think, I can think, we connect. Listening to Michele's songs, learn the lyrics, and singing with her will have a positive effect on your consciousness. Feeling is conscious awareness of vibration. You think in pictures. On a conscious or intellectual level, you transmit those pictures to other people through words, gestures, and writing. The heart is a term that the early Greeks used when referring to the subconscious mind. On a subconscious level, you communicate heart to heart through vibration. Your feelings are transmitted to other people through vibration. Air is made from the same stuff as the ground. Everything is energy in various states of vibration. Levels of vibration are referred to as frequencies. Both science and theology agree everything is the expression of one power that operates in an orderly manner more commonly referred to as law. Vibration is one of those exact laws of nature.

Read the law of vibration on page 110 in my book 'You Were Born Rich' again. Make sure you mean what you say, and you say what you mean. When you say one thing and are emotionally involved with the opposite you are sending both messages to the other person.

That sort of mental activity causes confusion in your mind and theirs. Those messages are called double binding messages and will never produce desired results. When two or more people come together on the same frequency of thought that creates synergy and synergy is hot energy. And let's not forget the beautiful truth, the whole universe is related, we are all part of the same family.

Risk

Bob:
Are you ready? Are you really ready? Then let's go. Open the door of your mind. You are going to take a Risk.

Bob, I'd love to take a risk but I'm scared. I'd give anything to leave this mental prison.

Bob:
Follow my lead and remember you are never alone. Risks must be taken because the greatest hazard in life is to Risk nothing. The person who risks nothing does nothing, has nothing, and is nothing. Only the person who risks is free.

All right. Never avoid Risk in favor of security. Helen Keller suggested that security is a myth. She said, "If life is not a series of risks, then it is nothing."

Hello, this is Bob Proctor with another great topic. This chapter on Risk will help you out of your comfort zone and set you free. It will add a splendid dimension of adventure and creativity to your life. Prepare to venture where you have never been before. Turn your life into one exciting adventure after another. Listen carefully now to the lyrics of this beautiful song we have written just for you that Michele adds life to. You will hear words of wisdom that are rich with truth words that will inspire you to take risks.

TheMysticalExperience.com/NPSongs

Risk opens the door to a magic place
It gives you courage and it gives you grace
You'll love; you'll learn, grow and be free
Come on take a risk, it's for you and me
Take a risk...everybody

Be bold, be brave
Stand straight and tall
Let the power flow
You're gonna win it all
Come on take a risk

In the magic place everybody's free
It's the spot your Spirit oh longs to be
When you risk, remember that you're not alone
So get up and out of your comfort zone
Take a risk... everybody

Be bold, be brave
Stand straight and tall
Let the power flow
You're gonna win it all
Come on take a risk

Take a risk to freedom
Freedom

You're going to the place we're homesick for
Freedom Freedom
Take a risk to freedom

My dictionary tells me to Risk is to expose oneself to the chance of loss. I suppose that is true. A piece of literature I was given suggested that to laugh is to Risk appearing the fool. To weep is to Risk appearing sentimental. To reach out to another is to Risk involvement. To express feelings is to Risk exposing your true self. To place your ideas, your dreams, before the crowd is to Risk their loss. To love is to Risk not being loved in return. To live is to Risk dying. To hope is to Risk despair. To try is to Risk failure.

But risks must be taken because the greatest hazard in life is to Risk nothing. The person who risks nothing does nothing, has nothing, and is nothing. You may avoid suffering and sorrow if you don't Risk but you simply cannot learn, feel, change, grow, love, or live. Only a person who risks is free. What causes individuals to shy away from taking a Risk even if it is a low Risk and will give them something they really want? Well, certainly high on most people's list would be the fear of loss, failure, and perceived humiliation if the loss were to occur.

I think we should start by realizing that the good we realize when we step out and take a Risk is only part of the gain. The real win is the confidence and experience we acquire which translates into new opportunities for growth, enjoyment, and expansion in all areas of our life. When you think of the word Risk what comes to mind? You must understand that Risk is not synonymous with gambling. Risk-taking is not gambling in any sense of the word. I have often said that the truly big winners in the world are the individuals who make decisions. They also take risks. But they do not view the decisions they have made as gambling.

The big winners in life are truly focused on where they are headed and what they are doing and typically they are involved in a really big idea. The big winners in life are confident. They never imagine that they'll fail. They are prepared to put everything into making it happen. Their energy, their time, their money, the list goes on and on. The average individual most certainly looks at their moves as enormous risks.

Over the years I have read, heard, and collected numerous human interest stories about extraordinary people. Stories that have inspired me to continue taking risks. Risks that have continued to set me free. Some time ago Jerry Robert, the author of 'Conquering Life's Obstacles' shared a story with me that I shall never forget. I want to share that story with you. It's a true story about a great risk-taker from Indiana in the United States of America. The man's name is Herman Krannert.

Go back with me to the year 1925. This story begins in Indianapolis. Herman Krannert was an executive with the Sefton Container Company. He was summoned to Chicago to have lunch with the president of the company. He was very excited and for good reason. He had never been invited to have lunch with the president before. Krannert met his president at the athletic club and while they were having lunch the president said, "Herman, I'm going to make an announcement in the company this afternoon that greatly impacts your life. We're going to promote you to senior executive vice president and you're going to be the newest member of the board of directors." Krannert was stunned. He said, "Mr. President, I had no idea I was even being considered for this. I want you to know that I'll be the most loyal employee this company has ever had. I'm going to dedicate my life to making this company the finest corporation in America."

The president was gratified by this and said, "You know, Herman, I'm glad you mentioned that because there's one thing, I'd like you to remember. As a member of the board of directors, you will vote exactly the way I tell you to vote." The president's command took the wind out of Hermit Krannert's sails. He said he wasn't sure that he could do that. "Come on, Herman, that's the way it is in the business world. I'm putting you on the board of directors. You'll do what I tell you, right?"

The more Herman thought about what the president had said the angrier he became. At the end of the lunch Herman Krannert stood up and said, "Mr. President, I want you to understand that I cannot accept this promotion. I will not be a puppet for anybody, on a board of directors, or anywhere else." Then, he added, "Not only that but I will not work for a company where such demands are made. I quit."

He came back to Indianapolis that night, approached his wife, and said, "You'll be excited to know that today I was promoted to executive vice president, I was made a member of the board of directors, and I quit." She said, "you quit? Have you lost your mind?" but when he told her what happened she was very supportive and said, "Well, I guess we'll have to find something else."

Four nights later a knock came at his door. Six senior executives from his company burst through the door all excited. "Herman, we heard what happened the other day. We think that's the greatest thing we've ever heard. In fact, we quit too."

"What do you mean you quit too?", Herman said.

"That's it, Herman. we quit too. and here's the good news, we're going to go to work for you."

"How are you going to work for me? I don't even have a job."

They replied, "Oh, we figure you'll find something, Herman. And when you do, we're going to work for you."

That night those seven people sat down at Herman Krannert's dining room table and created the Inland Container Corporation. An organization that exists because one man in 1925 refused to compromise his core beliefs. Herman Krannert found himself in a position where he was forced to make a major decision. His choice was obvious. Compromise his beliefs and live a lie, or Risk everything. What would you have done? What do you believe? What are your core beliefs? You must recognize them, and you must live by them as Herman Krannert did or you will never be free. You will be someone else's puppet.

I'm going to tell you what I believe. I believe in God. I believe in an all-powerful, ever-present, all-knowing presence that operates in a very exact manner, more commonly referred to by law. I believe this power will give me what I ask for every time and without exception. If I ask for the strength to walk where I have never been before the strength will be there when I need it. If I need a creative idea to solve a problem I will be inspired at the right moment. I believe in the Law Of Opposites. If you can see a negative situation, you know there is a positive hidden somewhere within the situation. And if you seek, you will find.

If Risk is to expose oneself to a chance of loss, by law you must also be exposing yourself to a win. However, you must keep in mind that the laws are exact and must be understood. The law of clarity or as we previously referred to it, the law of opposite, does not merely state that everything has an opposite. It is equal and opposite. If the Risk is small the win will be as well. However, the size of the Risk you take is not that important. What is important is that you absolutely refuse to play it safe. Taking small risks will lead to larger ones.

Michele, who does such a magnificent job singing and producing these songs, put it best the other day when she pointed out that big trees grow from small seeds. How true that is. Risk-taking should be a subject taught in school along with reading and mathematics, and it is a subject that could be taught. You can teach anyone anything. Unfortunately, very few people were taught anything constructive about risk-taking when they were children.

When we were children, our little ears were constantly hearing, "be careful, you might fall." what did they mean 'might fall'? We did fall. We're going to fall. Where the heck did they get this 'might' stuff from. Think of how much better equipped we would be to face life's challenges, and succeed regardless, if we had repetitively heard, "take a chance and don't worry about falling." because you're going to fall, often. Falling is an important part of learning. Many of the greatest lessons you will receive in life are going to come from falling, from your failures. Failing will never make you a failure unless you quit.

Unfortunately, very few people heard that when they were small. The vast majority of our population have been mentally programmed to play it safe. In my seminars, I have often said that a little baby is a natural-born risk-taker. The baby never considers the consequences of falling when it is learning to walk. Falling is acknowledged as a natural consequence of learning to walk. It is not gambling. Everyone knows that the baby will fall but that ultimately the baby will learn to walk. The baby, nor the baby's parents, never considered an option that the baby would not learn to speak or master a myriad of motor skills simply to avoid the stumbling the baby must endure.

What happens to us? Why do we enter the world one way and, for most people, leave another? Why is it that we do not see the process of reaching our goals as having steps similar to the ones the baby must take in order to learn to walk? There will be some stumbling and falling in the learning process, but success can only be reached when we are prepared to take those steps. All of them. Even the ones where we may fall down. You must constantly challenge yourself.

When I was a youngster in school I participated in track and field. Pole vaulting was my specialty. It was the one event I seem to do much better at than others. I clearly remember I knocked that crossbar flying more often than I cleared it. I also remember I was not a very enthusiastic kid when that happened. I suppose knocking the bar off left me with a feeling that I had failed, and as I remember no one advised me of anything different. Reflecting on those days I can clearly see those times would have been a tremendous opportunity for the teachers to help me understand one of life's greatest lessons, but it never happened.

It would be many years before I learned the truth the hard way. Reaching the goal is not success. Success is moving toward the goal. When I was knocking down the crossbar, I was attempting to reach the goal. I was stretching, giving everything I had. That could hardly be considered failing. Every time I tried to clear that bar; I was risking the ridicule of the other kids. I risked having them laugh at me when I missed, and they did laugh. They sure did.

Every time I ran down the field lowering the pole into the box trying to vault myself over the bar, I was challenging myself. Taking risks is essential when you want to reach a goal, and the purpose of goals is growth. When you challenge yourself, you are bringing more of yourself to the surface. If you knock the bar flying today at least you will know you're challenging yourself, towards your success.

Intellectually you know different, but it is not your intellectual mind that's controlling your behavior. That is determining the results you receive in life. Your behavior and your results are the expression of your conditioned subconscious mind. That part of your personality which is housing the ridiculous play-it-safe information which has been passed along from one generation to the next for too long. 97% of us are the product of someone else's way of thinking.

Make a decision right now to change. Decide this very moment there will be no more playing it safe. Just freedom from now on. No more 'saving it for a rainy day' type of thinking in your life. When people get caught up in the habit of 'saving for a rainy day' that's generally what they get, a rainy day. Let it go, take a Risk. Open the doors of your mind and step out where the sun shines. Make magic. No more rainy days. You may get some liquid sunshine but no more rainy days. If you dream of living your life in a really big way you must accept risk-taking as a very real part of the apprenticeship that you must serve.

Have you sat back lately completely relaxed, mentally played with the idea of what you plan to do with the rest of your life? If you haven't it's a great exercise. This is a fascinating world, and you have what would appear to be almost magical powers locked up within you. You can actually call your own shots, do your own bidding. In truth, there is nothing holding you back.

I clearly remember the first time I heard a motivational recording by the late Earl Nightingale. His words lit a fire inside of me which grows brighter every day. Earl told a story about a farmer who's out walking in a field. He looked down and saw a tiny pumpkin growing on a vine. Nearby he spotted a small glass jar.

The farmer reached down and placed a tiny pumpkin inside of the small jar. The pumpkin continued to grow until it filled the inside of the jar beyond which it could not grow. There are a number of people like that tiny pumpkin. They limit themselves. They refuse to take a risk. They never truly test the strength of their abilities.

One of my favorite authors is Gurdjieff. He wrote, 'The first reason for man's inner slavery is his ignorance and above all is ignorance of himself. Without self-knowledge, without understanding the workings and function of his machine man cannot be free. He cannot govern himself. He will always remain a slave, the plaything of forces acting upon him. This is why in all ancient teachings the first demand at the beginning of the way to liberation was to *know thyself*.

Know thyself is liberating advice, there's just absolutely no question about it. Imagine that you have been dealt five cards in a card game. The cards are lying on the table in front of you, but you don't know what cards you're playing with before you pick them up and look at the other side to see what you've been dealt. Life is much like a game of cards. It's not until you look at the other side of yourself, the inside, that you know what you have to work with. Know thyself.

Here's a marvelous piece of literature on Risk and resistance which was written by the late William Penn Patrick. Listen real close as I share this with you because I've grown to love it.

"No person, ideal, or institution becomes great until Great Resistance has been encountered. Greatness cannot be achieved until this concept is understood.

Unfortunately, the average person is ignorant of this rule to achievement. Mr. And Miss Average, in their ignorance, are fearful and reluctant to encounter even slight resistance. They don't want to make waves or be criticized, and they incorrectly feel that criticism will hold them back and prevent their happiness from being realized. In truth, the opposite is the case.

Take note: when we begin to change, we are first given resistance by our loved ones, for they fear change because change means facing the unknown. When we begin to make rapid progress or commitment to rapid progress, we have roadblocks thrown up by our friends and relatives. They begin to resist by negative comments and actions which are devices to cause you to maintain the status quo.

Now, if you are to achieve great progress, you must prevail against those closest to you. this is difficult and requires courage because you desire to please and not hurt those you love. The truth is that great harm befalls your loved ones when you fail to be yourself, to do your thing, and become what you are meant to become. This is so because you lose your enthusiasm for life. Your growth process stops, and your self-esteem diminishes. Those negatives are reversed when you stand your ground and when you have prevailed, your loved ones gain a new and higher respect for you. History records countless events which prove the point.

We are fortunate to have such great resistance. This resistance is evidence of our greatness, and it provides us with the energy to prevail, to conquer, and to dominate. These next few short years will record a brilliant history and establish a permanent place for our way of life – which is Freedom to be and to work out our dreams for a great world, for ourselves, for children, and all of mankind.

Understand our battle and be glorified that you are a part of the making of history. The work you do today will provide new freedom and hope for millions yet to come."

Take a moment and mentally thank the memory of William Penn Patrick for those beautiful words of wisdom. Thousands of men and women have been inspired to keep on keeping on from what he shared with us. By reviewing those words frequently until they become resident in your subconscious mind you'll be inspired as well. I want to suggest that you think of where you are in life, the success you are enjoying. Think of what it took you to get where you are. Whatever it took to get you to the point you're at will not be sufficient to keep you there. No one ever arrives. The risks and resistance never ends if you are going to improve your position, and you're either improving your position or you're sliding backwards. How often have you watched successful people fall from grace after reaching the pinnacle of their selected career?

You need to keep pursuing, keep on doing, and looking for new and better ways to grow, to change, to expand beyond the position that you've reached. You just must keep taking risks. I'm not speaking here of change for change's sake, but rather for the sake of growth. It matters not how much we change provided we are changing, risking, improving, and growing. To continue with positive and dynamic motion in our personal or family and business lives, we need a track to run on. We need to ask ourselves deep, penetrating questions frequently as a constant checkup. Answering these questions honestly will make you aware that your life can make a difference, a big difference.

You have the talent and ability along with an infinite source of potential to develop yourself into something great, to do work that really counts. The real key to living a fulfilled life lies in doing great work. However, great work is always preceded by many risks.

George Bernard Shaw said, "This is the true joy in life, being used for a purpose recognized by yourself as a mighty one. Being a force of nature instead of a feverish, selfish little clod of ailments and grievances, complaining that the world will not devote itself to making you happy."

Shaw's quote should be posted in every workplace, home, and school. I clearly remember a talk I heard many years ago in Chicago when I worked with the late Earl Nightingale. Earl was speaking at a meeting that we were conducting. He said that we were quickly reaching a point where we almost deified leisure time. He went on to say that he felt that was rather sad because all of our real pleasure comes from our labor, not our leisure. Work's made for us; we're not made for work. Think, really think. Your greatest feeling of satisfaction is always following some great Risk.

Make up your mind today to do work that counts. Step out of your comfort zone. Do it right now. The particular Risk you are contemplating may cause fear. You may be scared. Clearly understand there's nothing wrong with being scared. Everyone is full of fear from time to time however we must never permit being scared to stop us. Often, we find people who are scared of the dark. Some people are scared of meeting strangers. That may sound silly, and in truth being scared is silly, but nevertheless fear is real. Its cause is ignorance.

Today there are thousands of people who are scared of losing their jobs or their businesses. What should we do when we're scared? Well, I picked up some great advice from a magazine I subscribe to each month. 'Do it scared.' That's right. Do it scared. Refuse to permit this negative demon to control you, your emotions or your actions.

Eleanor Roosevelt put it well. She said, "You gain strength, courage, and confidence by every experience in which you really stop to look fear right in the face." By following her advice you will liberate yourself from this crippling emotional state that being scared causes. Burn this idea deep in your marvelous mind. You can accomplish whatever you can visualize. If you're a parent, make certain that you inundate the little mind in your care with this concept. When they are grown, they will thank you a million times and their children will as well.

While we are thinking about children let's throw up a caution flag. There is a four-letter word that most parents use around their children so frequently that the children pick it up, and before too long it's buried in the treasury of their subconscious mind. The four-letter word is can't.

This word has done more damage than all the other frowned-upon four-letter words put together. Can't is a word that paralyzes any constructive progress. It switches your mind into a negative frequency. It is a four-letter word that will open your mind to a never-ending flow of logical, practical reasons which will enable you to justify why you are not able to do something you sincerely want to accomplish.

The only alternative to that four-letter word is its polar opposite. I can. I can is far more important than IQ. You don't necessarily have to be very smart to win but you must be willing. To assist you in preparing for a life of Risk and adventure permit me to summarize 20 key points.

1. Risk must be taken because the greatest hazard in life is to Risk nothing.
2. You may avoid suffering and sorrow if you don't Risk but you simply cannot learn, feel, change, grow, love, or live.

3. Only a person who risks is free.
4. Understand that Risk is not synonymous with gambling.
5. What are your core beliefs? You must recognize them, and you must live by them.
6. If Risk is to expose oneself to a chance of loss, by law you must also be exposing yourself to a win.
7. Big trees grow from small seeds.
8. Failing will never make you a failure unless you quit.
9. Reaching the goal is not success. Success is moving toward the goal.
10. When people get caught up in the habit of saving for a rainy day that is generally what they get - a rainy day.
11. Gurdjieff said, "The first reason for man's inner slavery is his ignorance and above all his ignorance of himself."
12. No person, idea, or institution becomes great until great resistance has been encountered.
13. When we begin to take real risks, we are first given resistance by our loved ones.
14. When you take the risks and when you have prevailed, your loved ones gain a new and a higher respect for you.
15. Whatever it took to get you to the point you're at will not be sufficient to keep you there.

16. George Bernard Shaw said, "This is the true joy in life, being used for a purpose recognized by yourself as a mighty one."
17. Earl nightingale said we are quickly reaching a point where we almost deify leisure time. He went on to say that that was rather sad because all of our pleasure comes from our labor not our leisure.
18. Burn this idea deep in your marvelous mind. You can accomplish whatever you can visualize.
19. Can't is a word that paralyzes any constructive progress. Replace it with its polar opposite. I can, which is more important than IQ.
20. And last but certainly not least. The beautiful truth which was given to us by Helen Keller. "Security is a myth. If life is not a series of risks, then it is nothing."

And now before I give you the information of how to find out more about what we're doing in this company of ours I want you to listen to our Risk song again. I want you to memorize the lyrics. Let Michele's voice echo in your brain because the lyrics are going to help you go where you want to go. Listen carefully.

RISK LYRICS

Risk opens the door to a magic place
It gives you courage and it gives you grace
You'll love; you'll learn, grow and be free
Come on take a risk, it's for you and me
Take a risk...everybody

Be bold, be brave
Stand straight and tall
Let the power flow
You're gonna win it all
Come on take a risk

In the magic place everybody's free
It's the spot your Spirit oh longs to be
When you risk, remember that you're not alone
So get up and out of your comfort zone
Take a risk... everybody

Be bold, be brave
Stand straight and tall
Let the power flow
You're gonna win it all
Come on take a risk
Take a risk to freedom
Freedom
You're going to the place we're homesick for
Freedom
Take a risk to freedom

Persistence

In 1953 a beekeeper from Auckland, New Zealand earned world recognition with fame and fortune to follow. Knighted by Queen Elizabeth for his accomplishments, Sir Edmund Hillary, and his native guide Tenzing Norgay became the first two people to climb Mount Everest and safely return after having tried and failed on two previous attempts. Hillary had two obvious character strengths which literally took him to the very top, vision and Persistence. Without Persistence, all his skills would have meant nothing.

These qualities and characteristics are the same as those you need to lead you to the top of your mountain. You are confronted by mountains every day. You can either climb the mountains or remain in the foothills. Any successful person will tell you that Persistence is absolutely essential to climbing the mountains. The individuals who remain in the foothills have never chosen to develop this strength. These people dream of being stars. They want to receive the fame and fortune, but fame is not a common suitor. Fame only comes calling after a high price has been paid and the poor people who march in the foothills refuse to pay that price.

Napoleon Hill wrote in his book 'Think And Grow Rich,' "There may be no heroic connotation to the word Persistence, but the quality is to the character of the human being what carbon is to steel." Hill was right. Persistence is a unique mental strength. A strength which is essential to combat the fierce power of repeated rejections and numerous other obstacles that sit in waiting and are all a part of winning in a fast-moving, ever-changing world.

There are hundreds of biographies of highly successful men and women who have cut a path for others to follow while leaving their mark on the scrolls of history. Every one of these great individuals were Persistent. In many cases, it was the only quality which separated them from everyone else.

Consider Ben Hogan. He weighed only 135 pounds, but every ounce was saturated with Persistence. Born into a poor family, Hogan began to caddy at a local golf club as a boy to earn extra money for his family. This led to the birth of a dream. He would become a great golfer. Through a great deal of hard work practice and Persistence, Ben Hogan became one of the world's greatest golfers. In 1948 he won the United States Open Championship. His accomplishments earned him world recognition, but he had not yet faced his mountain. The next year Hogan was involved in a head-on collision with a bus, and he was not expected to survive his injuries. He did, but the doctor said he would never walk again. That was their opinion, not Ben Hogan's.

He insisted his golf clubs be put in the corner of his hospital room as he began to visualize himself playing golf again. One year later Hogan won the United States Open Championship again. The next year he won three major championships. In all 54 of his victories followed that near-tragic accident. Does Persistence pay? Ask Ben Hogan.

I had the pleasure of speaking to a group of businesspeople in Fort Worth, Texas many years ago. The meeting I was addressing was held at the Colonial Golf and Country Club. This is Ben Hogan's home club. Prior to my speech, I had the good fortune of seeing the 54 trophies Ben Hogan had earned after his tragic accident. The trophies are there on display to encourage the weak-minded and to remind and reinforce the strong.

Another person who has aptly demonstrated how far Persistence can take you is Charlie Boswell. Boswell is a Birmingham, Alabama businessman, salesman, author, and golfer. He holds numerous national and international golf championships. But what really distinguishes him is that he is blind. That's right. Charlie

Boswell lost his sight after being blown off a tank in the second world war. Selling, golfing, and writing are all the pursuits Boswell has engaged in since his tragic mishap. Do you think Charlie Boswell is persistent? Well, do you? If you were to compare an entrepreneurial or sales career to any in the entertainment industry, you would find that every actor or actress holds a dream of becoming a star. Every entrepreneur salesperson holds a similar dream. However, as an entrepreneur or as a salesperson you have much greater control over your destiny.

There's no capricious director or casting agent who can put their foot on the brake of your progress. You alone decide to quit or to continue when those inevitable mountains loom up on the road to your goal. Every industry has entrepreneurs and salespeople. After every star there are at least twenty amateurs. 20% of the salespeople take home 80% of the commissions. The beautiful aspect of sales is that you decide to which percent you will belong. And in the final analysis as an entertainer, you must keep this beautiful truth firmly planted in your mind, that even the capricious directors and casting agents of our world are always overruled by the laws of our universe. Whatever you can conceive and believe, through Persistence, you must achieve.

Entrepreneurial situation or not, decide right now to be one of those people who make it happen. To be one of the group who receives the lion's share of the profits. Understand that to join this select group of big producers you must begin your Persistence exercises now. Make Persistence your most well-developed mental muscle. Persistence cannot be replaced by any other quality. Superior skills will not make up for it. A well-rounded, formal education cannot replace it. Nor will calculated plans nor a magnetic personality. When you are persistent you will become a leader in your industry.

I picked up a piece of literature years ago which illustrates that point perfectly. Let me share it with you. It was written by Calvin Coolidge. It's called 'Persistence'. "Nothing in the world can take the place of Persistence. Talent will not. Nothing is more common than unsuccessful people with talent. Genius will not. Unrewarded genius is almost a proverb. Education will not. The world is full of educated derelicts. Persistence and determination alone are omnipotent. The slogan 'Press on' has solved and always will solve the problems of the human race."

The people who never tackled a mountain who perpetually wander in the foothills most of their lives have, in my opinion, lied to themselves and everyone else who would listen so often and for so long that they are no longer even aware of what they are doing. They say they are content with their results. They will say that climbing a mountain is not important to them. That they are getting by just fine the way they are. Odds are they secretly started to climb the mountain years ago and got scared. They hit the terror barrier, quickly retreated to the comfort zone, and have been hiding behind their own false rationale ever since. They frequently justify their sick, mediocre performance with statements like, "Why should I go all out? When I get there the boss will just want more." These poor, non-productive individuals are lost, or at best misguided.

If you are not able to wake them up, make certain that you do not permit them to pull you into their trap. In fact, when you come in contact with these poor souls let them serve as a triggering mechanism to mentally double your commitment to yourself to become more persistent. My Webster dictionary has this to say about Persistence, "To continue especially in spite of opposition or difficulty.' Boleh, Boleh. (Yes Yes)

To this point, I have had quite a lot to say about Persistence. Those who have developed it and the necessity for Persistence. But there's something missing in this message. How to.

How do you become persistent? That's a good question.

Persistence is never developed by accident. You are not born with it, and you cannot inherit it. And there is no one in the entire world that can develop Persistence for you. Persistence is as interwoven with success as the chicken is with the egg. And I'm talking about real success, as it's covered in the chapter we made on success.

Ultimately Persistence becomes a way of life, but that's not where it begins. To develop the mental strength of Persistence you must first want something. You have to want something so much that it becomes a heated desire, a passion in your belly. You must fall in love with the idea, yes literally fall in love with the idea. Magnetize yourself to every part of the idea. Then Persistence will be automatic. The very idea of not persisting will become hateful and anyone who even attempted to take your dream away from you or stop you or even slow you down would be in serious trouble. Difficulties, obstacles, and mountains will definitely appear and on a regular basis, but because of your Persistence, they will be defeated by you every time.

All right. Where does this leave you? It leaves you at the crossroads that every self-help book, every motivation program, and every seminar leads to. You must decide what you want, what you really want, way down deep inside or you'll remain in the foothills surrounded by losers.

This is a subject I have studied over all my adult life, and I can tell you one thing, very few people have admitted to themselves that this is what I want. This is what I really want, and I'm prepared to give my life for it. That last statement may cause you to sit up and say, "Wait a minute." And that's fine. But you should seriously think about it. Because you are already giving your life for what you are doing. What are you doing? What are you trading your life for? Are you making a fair trade? Remember, whatever you are doing was your decision. Or was it? Or was it? You could possibly be one of those poor people who have been wandering in the foothills leaving the decisions of where you are going and what you are doing with your life to other people.

Just following, always following. That is where most people live. If that is the case, that's OK. Don't let it bother you for one more valuable second of your life. Forgive yourself and that way of life. Just let it go forever. Treat this message on Persistence as your wake-up call. This red hot message on Persistence will help you get out of the foothills and lead you to the very top of the mountain all the way to the summit. It's not a chair lift, it will not make the climb any easier. You'll still attract the necessary problems and they'll come to strengthen you, but this message will definitely make the climb to the top of the mountain a lot more fun. It will also help you develop the granite strong attitude, the certainty, the inner knowing that you will get to the top. The summit will be yours and the view from the top is going to be awesome. It will be reward enough for all the problems that you encountered to get there.

Talking about summits and Persistence let's go back and think about Ed Hillary. What kind of a passion do you suppose he felt for his goal? He must have truly wanted to climb that mountain. Think of the physical and mental abuse he was subjecting himself to. He was obviously prepared to give his life for what he wanted. Every person who had ever seriously attempted to climb Everest, as far back as our history records go, shows they either failed miserably or experienced a tragic death trying.

Most people, when they think about Sir Edmund Hillary and his expeditions, ask what kept him going year after year. He wanted. That's what kept him going. That is why he was persistent. He wanted, really wanted at a gut level, wanted something enough to keep going. When a person does not understand that they'll usually ask, "Why? Why did he want it?" he didn't know why. He didn't have to know why. Why wasn't important. Want was important.

Persistent people never know why they want. They only know that they want, and they must have it. And to have it they must do. And to do they must be. And they want it so much that they keep imaging. Seeing it as if it has already happened. Until they become the living breathing embodiment of whatever the want represents. For those are steps which must be followed for the creative process to work in our life. Ed Hillary became the mountain climber.

The why's in our life are a blessing from Spirit. Let me repeat that. The why's in our life are a blessing from Spirit. They are Spirit's way of turning us into a perfect instrument for Spirit to express itself through. Spirit is always for expansion and fuller expression. The essence of you is Spiritual. Spirit is saying to your consciousness, "Here. Want this. Really want it."

When you want this enough you'll grow into the person who is capable of doing great work. You are worthy of having whatever you want. That is why ordinary people have always done extraordinary work. Because listen closely, this is one of the greatest liberating truths you will ever hear. The ordinary people did extraordinary things because they consciously recognized what they wanted, and they refused to suppress or dismiss it. They would not let it go even if failure, rejection, bankruptcy, or death was staring them in the face. It would have to be that way, or the ordinary person would never do the extraordinary. They would never persist. The power of their want and the intensity of their Persistence caused them to draw on resources they previously were not aware they possessed. They expressed what they had within. Greatness.

TheMysticalExperience.com/NPSongs

When the want is weak, you'll quit at the first obstacle. The proper want is essential to Persistence. This concept of wants and the why's is dealt with in greater depth on success. Get it and study it because a proper understanding of these concepts will virtually guarantee you a successful life. The playthings like cars, houses, and money will automatically come to you. They rarely represent real success.

Come with me as we review Ben Hogan, a very ordinary young fellow. He became such an absolutely extraordinary inspiration to millions of people. In one line the answer is obvious. He had a dream. Every time I think of people like Hogan and Hillary and their dreams, I think of what another very ordinary man who has done an extraordinary thing said about situations like this. "If the dream is big enough the facts don't count." Sam Kalenuik said that, and he knows what he's talking about. Sam is a good friend and one of the owners of Matol Botanical, an extraordinary company which has helped hundreds of thousands of people.

It is too easy just to say that Ben Hogan had a dream. Ben Hogan's dream had become an obsession. Ben was not using the dream. Possibly in the very early stages, he was, but not for long. No, the dream was using Ben. The great psychologist Alfred Adler nailed it when he said, "I am grateful to the idea that has used me."

I love that. I really do. The very idea of Persistence filled every cell of Ben Hogan's being but that was because his want was so strong. Remember Persistence is the real focus of this message. It's important that we keep that in mind because we could very easily get lost climbing Mount Everest with Ed Hillary or playing golf with Hogan. They're not the stars of this movie, they're playing a supporting role. Persistence is the star. Properly digested in your mind Persistence will make you a star. It'll give you that number one hit worldwide.

How does an idea, a want, a dream get such a grip on a person that Persistence becomes a natural outgrowth of it? Napoleon Hill explained this very well. Hill said, at first the idea, the want has to be coaxed, nursed, and enticed just to remain alive but gradually the idea will take on a power of its own and sweep aside all opposition. It will then coax, nurse, and drive you.

He went on to explain that ideas are like that. They have more power than the physical brains that gave birth to them. They have the power to live on long after the physical brain that's created them has turned to dust. Wow. Isn't that beautiful? This is not a verbatim quotation, but I know it's accurate. I have studied Napoleon Hill's philosophy for over 30 years. That's what happened to Ben Hogan. I guess if the truth were known Ben Hogan did not have much of a choice.

Years before he had turned his will over to the idea of becoming the greatest golfer in the world. Nothing could shake Hogan loose from that idea. His entire mental being was directed toward doing whatever was required for that idea to move into physical form. Have you decided what you want? Is your want that strong? It is almost a waste of time attempting to develop Persistence if the want is not there. The problems of life will defeat you.

It's a well-known and documented fact that the problems in life are numerous, they come frequently. And are often giants. But yes, there is a but, when the dream is big enough the problems will be beaten, and the facts won't count. Sam is right. I really do love that and I must remember to thank Sam Kalenuik every chance I get for teaching me that beautiful truth. Think about it. When someone presents you with a fact, a big, bad, negative fact which shows you, what proves to you why you can't do what your heart tells you what you must do, you can do as I do. Smile at the carrier and quietly remember what Sam said. My dream is so big that fact doesn't count then persist.

Come back to Ben Hogan and you'll understand better what Sam meant. Ben Hogan was in a head-on collision in his car. He saw it coming and could not prevent it. His wife was in the front seat of the car with him. In an attempt to protect her, which he did, he threw himself in front of her. Ben's body was crushed. The police who came to the scene thought he was dead. There was debris all over the highway. The debris included his golf clubs which were strewn all over the place. When they were putting Hogan in the ambulance, Mrs. Hogan asked a police officer if he would please pick up Ben's golf clubs for her. The officer looked at her and replied, "Lady, he's not going to need these sticks anymore." Mrs. Hogan quickly advised the policeman that he obviously did not know who he had just put in the ambulance.

When they got Ben to the hospital, he was alive but not expected to live. The best doctors in the country were flown in to operate on him. It was their opinion that if he lived, he most certainly would never walk again. Ben Hogan did live. He insisted that his golf clubs be placed in the hospital room where he could see them. He then demanded that an exercise bar be rigged up over his bed. This was in spite of the fact that he could not even move his arms let alone lift his body.

Do you remember what Sam Kalenuik said about facts and dreams? The hospital staff brought in the exercise bar just to humor him. They felt sorry for him. Negative facts versus wants, dreams, Persistence. Now you know what will win. The dream, of course, every time.

One year to the day from the date of the accident Ben Hogan tied one of the greatest golfers who has ever played the game and is still playing the game in a tournament. Sam Sneed. A tournament that many golfers dropped out of because of driving rain. Ben Hogan went on to write his name in the history books of golf by winning 54 major tournaments after that accident. Think of what persistence did for Ben Hogan. It saved his life. It gave him life.

Persistence will save your life. It'll give you life. If you're having trouble with persistence your want is probably puny. It isn't big enough. This is probably the cause of your problem. Look around, it's a common problem. It's a human problem. Lack of Persistence is almost always a symptom of the real problem. You must give these two concepts priority in your life: Wants and Persistence. Your life will be shallow if this is not given top priority. You'll live like minnows in the shallows. I want to entice you to come out here in the deep waters of life. The view is spectacular. The people you meet are tremendous. They are focused, dynamic, creative individuals. The energy is hot, hot, hot. Persistence will, as the lyrics of the song promise, cause you to express what you've got. And when you do that, fame, which is not a common suitor, will most certainly have your number and will come calling. Fortune will be yours to hold. Oh yes, it will. Now listen to this and grasp the truth of what you're about to hear.

Fame & fortune stand there waiting
They will never fade away
They're both yours for the asking
But there's a price you need to pay

It's PERSISTENCE...PERSISTENCE
That shovels up the gold
It's persistence, yes persistence

That brings fame for you to hold

Fame is not a common suitor
And fortune's fickle I am told
You must develop that one ingredient
Or you're alone out in the cold

It's persistence, yes persistence
That expresses what you've got
It's persistence, yes persistence
That makes fame & fortune both so hot

You beat resistance with persistence
You stay until the job is done
Your reward will be fulfillment
You'll know inside that you have won

With persistence, persistence
I'll go the distance every time
With persistence, yes persistence
If I want it then it's mine

Isn't that great? The lyrics of our song say it all. I wonder if the people in the foothills would grasp the truth in this song. Let me repeat these lyrics. "You beat resistance with Persistence." The poor people in the foothills have not learned that. Resistance keeps beating them, causing them to whine and blame. They have not learned that they are the only problem they will ever have. Because of their losing 'I feel sorry for me', 'this is why it won't work' attitude they never stay until the job is done. They quit. They are beaten.

Listen to the next line. "Your reward will be fulfillment." Fulfillment? Fulfillment? The poor people in the foothills have never experienced the glory of fulfillment. Their reward? They never get rewarded. Ask them. They'll tell you they're always being taken advantage of. It's 'poor me'.

And then the line, "You'll know inside that you have won." Know inside? The people in the foothills don't go inside. They're too consumed by what is going on outside. Those other people cause the problems that they're faced with. "It's Proctor's fault or Sam Kalenuik's." They just don't understand. I have had the people in the foothills look me square in the eye and tell me, "Bob, you don't understand, do you? You just refuse to look at the figures."

Zigfield from Ziegfeld Follies said, "People that count are unhappy people." It's Persistence. Persistence. That's it. Make your want big and you will persist. Try to convince the person in the foothills that you are not doing what you are doing for fame and fortune. That you are doing it for fulfillment, and they'll shake their heads. They firmly believe that you are lying. Fame and fortune are nice, and they'll help you increase your physical comfort, and it will probably contribute to your creativity. But the real reward is fulfillment. It's knowing inside and knowing that you know.

Oh yes, it's definitely fulfillment. Have you got it? Really sing it along with Michele.
Decide what you truly want, and you will be persistent. Remember what Sam said, "If the want is big enough the facts don't count." And also remember what Napoleon Hill said, "There may be no heroic connotation to the word Persistence, but the quality is to the character of the human being what carbon is to steal." Go and do it. Study success. Choose what you want and persist. Life will then be what it's meant to be.

Action

TheMysticalExperience.com/NPSongs

Action Song Lyrics

Don't force it
Reinforce it
It's the expression of an impression
It's Action

Gonna find a real gold mine
Gonna find a real gold mine
With action, I know it's happened

Gonna find a real gold mine
Gonna find a real gold mine
With action, I know it's happened

I'm letting go of doubt and fear
I'm Letting in a good idea
With Action I know it's happened.

Gonna find a real gold mine
Gonna find a real gold mine
With ACTION

Action is a great word, isn't it? If you were thinking of words that were motivational action would have to be up near the top of the list. And on this topic, we want to add new meaning to action.

I'm letting go of doubt and fear
Letting in a good idea
With Action I know it's happened

I'm letting go of doubt and fear
Letting in a good idea
With action I know it's happened
Creative Action

Gonna find a real gold mine
Gonna find a real gold mine
With action, I know it's happened

Hello, this is Bob Proctor with your topic today on Action. In a movie you'll hear the director calling for Action. The camera begins to roll, things begin to happen. Used in the context of war it can have a very negative sting. You frequently hear of individuals being wounded or killed in Action. In this message Action is being used as a power principle. A very positive power principle. We want the concept of Action to play a very positive role in your life.

My Webster's dictionary has a number of different meanings for the word Action. The process of doing, that is the definition most people would focus their attention on. I want to suggest you put a different twist on the word Action. Make it a principle which gives you power. Make a decision to develop a reputation of a person that has outrageous Action. A person who makes the big moves. A person who gets big things done. When you want to go on a trip for your vacation make it worthwhile. Go around the world. Make the trip a memorable one.

If the Action is to improve your business, double your business. When you call for Action make it explosive Action so that the big moves are not something that other people are always involved in. You become one of those other people. You will, from time to time, hear an individual referred to as a person of great faith. It is wise to remember that faith without Action is useless. Gerda the German philosopher has been quoted as saying, "Before you can do something you must first be something." And of course, Gerda was right. Doing is the expression of what has already taken place mentally.

It is the expression of an impression. Action and doing are synonymous. When they are used in this context however the word Action adds an explosive dimension to the process of doing. Think of it for a moment. If I had said this principle is on doing, it would sound weak when compared to Action. Action is a power word. When you move into Action on an idea you are involved in the final stages of creation insofar as that idea is concerned take place. Action is not something that should be focused on or forced. Action should be automatic. Keep in mind Action is the physical expression of a higher activity.

Permit me to use the writing of this principle as an example. Writing and recording this Action lesson are just some of the many projects I am working on. I have mentally been working on this action principle for some time in different parts of the world, a few minutes here and there while I travel from one city to another. Or perhaps while I watch a football game I may mentally move over and give some energy to this lesson. I had a long day yesterday. I was up early after doing a number of projects at home. I went out and conducted a Born Rich seminar in Toronto. I returned home last evening and visited with my son and his family then when they left my wife and I watched Robert Redford's movie 'The River Runs Through It.' prior to going to bed I spoke with my assistant, Gina, who is presently in our office in Kuala Lumpur. I mention these events to provide you with the insight to realize I was tired. When I went to bed it was approximately 11:30 pm and I had completed a full, busy day. But at 3:00 am I awoke and was wide awake. The Action lesson was ready for Action.

I had been pregnant with this idea for the necessary period of time. It was ready. The Action lesson was about to be expressed. It was ready to be written. I attempted, when I realized what time, it was, to forget it and go back to sleep. It was no use and besides I knew better. I went to the kitchen, put on a pot of coffee, and began to write. The Action step becomes automatic when you prepare yourself mentally and when your ideas are ready for Action they should not be denied. The Action step in the creative process is the expression of an impression.

I spent a number of years working with the late Earl Nightingale. He was a wise man and he taught me many important lessons, one of which fits this lesson perfectly. He said ideas are like slippery fish. If you don't gaff them with the point of a pencil, they will probably get away and never come back. That is a beautiful truth worthy of serious consideration. Over the years' experience has taught me many lessons. I have come to the conclusion that, as a people, we are far too regimented in our behavior. Literally millions of potentially great individuals permit the clock to control their life and they pay an enormous price for it. They do not eat when they are hungry or sleep when they are tired. They do both when the clock or their mental conditioning dictates.

My mind had composed this lesson. It was ready to be written and it was ready to move onto the physical plane of life. It did not matter whether it was 3:00 am or 3:00 pm. I was ready to give birth to the idea. Had I stayed in bed until 8:00 or 9:00 am, as Earl Nightingale mentioned, many important parts of this lesson could very easily have swam downstream completely out of my reach. When you are mentally pregnant with a big idea keep this principle in mind, Action is the expression of an impression. Action comes when the idea is ready not when a clock dictates.

Have you noticed the real professionals in every walk of life are not clock watchers nor are they controlled or guided by the dictates of the masses. When they are ready for Action they act. They understand the birth of ideas and the birth of babies are governed by exactly the same laws. Examine what I have just shared with you. Think, really think. There is only one all-knowing, creative power in this universe. This power expresses itself in many ways, but it always works the same way. By law every form of creation is by law.

When a person is carrying a baby in the womb she is referred to as being pregnant with a new child. To make certain she carries the baby to full term and has a healthy birth there are certain rules which must be followed. Rest, relaxation, physical exercise, freedom from worry or stress, proper diet or nutrition, are all considerations to which a responsible mother gives high priority. And let's keep this basic truth in mind, when the time for the birth of the baby arrives nothing, absolutely nothing but the birth receives mum's attention. I should probably add complete and undivided attention. You just try and get her to go back to sleep or go for a cup of coffee or watch tv you know how successful you will be.

Here is another point you might want to remember. When the time arrives for the birth to take place the only people the mother wants in her life at that particular time are those people who are capable, competent, and to want to give their undivided attention to assisting in the birth of the child. Long after the child has been safely delivered and mum is completely rested from her flurry of creative activity a little idle chatter with a few non-productive possibly scatter-brained acquaintances or relatives would probably be tolerated, but even then, almost everyone's attention is attracted back to the magnificence of the newly arrived creation. New creations generally attract almost everyone's attention and admiration. The supreme satisfaction which many people miss out on in life comes only to those main contributors who work in harmony with the creator for the physical manifestation of the new creation. I have always felt that a mother receives a degree of satisfaction which a father will never completely understand. Their contribution to the birth of the child seems so much greater.

Now, let's move back to the explosive word Action. You want to be recognized or thought of as a person of Action. I'm sure you do and so you should. You are a creative expression of life. You have been endowed with the mental tools that enable you to work in harmony with the ever-present, all-powerful, all-knowing creator. So far as we know you are the only form of life which has been given those marvelous, mental powers. The nucleus of your being is perfect. It is always longing for expansion and fuller expression. You are capable of great work. We were never meant to spend our days involved in idle chatter or meaningless activity. It is our responsibility to grow, to develop a greater awareness, to enjoy every good imagined.

If you haven't already got a dynamite idea running around your mind, adding dimensions of joy and enthusiasm to your days, quit whatever you are doing right now. Lay back, relax, and permit your imagination to move. Begin to look from within to the source of unlimited supply. Look at your work. How can you improve what you are doing? How can you make it ten times, fifty times better? Don't worry about getting paid for it that will come, it must come, that is the law. Write your ideas down as they come to you. Do the same thing with your social life then go to your family life. Begin to imagine beautiful trips that you can take for your next vacation.

I began writing this as I have already mentioned in my own home at 3:00 am in the morning in Toronto, Canada. However, I left Toronto later that same day. At this moment it is 3:29 in the afternoon and I am in Kuala Lumpur, Malaysia living in the Duta Vista Executive Suites. What I am experiencing here everyone should experience at least once in their life. I flew into Malaysia from America with Malaysia Airlines, which in my opinion provide the very best service worldwide in air travel. The Duta Vista Executive Suites should never be considered a hotel. I have lived in hotels for 25 years. The Duta Vista is a dimension above the finest hotels. Everyone gets a suite, and they treat you like family. I absolutely love it here. Come to the Duta Vista on your next vacation and we'll have dinner together at the poolside restaurant.

Now that could be an idea that you can work on. Nine out of ten people would probably smile when they hear this and then think that would be nice, but you become the one in ten who smiles and then imagines yourself sharing dinner with me at the poolside restaurant. If you keep visualizing that idea it will become automatic. The Action will actually become automatic. Make it happen and I'm serious. Fax the Duta Vista for information. Their fax number in Kuala Lumpur is +032550808.

Phone Malaysia Airlines right now and book your trip. Make it first class, you deserve the very best, and Malaysia Airlines has the best. I don't care if you have to book your trip for one year from today, book it.

John Canary suggested to Randy Lefleur what I have just suggested to you. Randy is a ReMax real estate agent in Toronto, Canada. Randy and Colleen, his girlfriend, had lunch with John and I today at the Duta Vista poolside restaurant. Randy took Action on a big idea. He and Colleen are on their way around the world. They are people of Action. That is possibly why Randy is one of the top real estate agents in Canada. Remember positive action is preceded by emotional involvement which comes from the impression upon your universal subconscious mind. Build the image and keep thinking about it continually. Give it the energy it will require to sustain life.

You are probably aware that millions of ideas are either aborted prior to birth or are stillborn. Negative suggestions from ignorant but well-meaning people coupled together with doubt and worry and possibly envy is generally what takes the life out of most great ideas. Just as the expectant mother must care for the unborn child, she carries you must care for the unborn idea you carry. Associate with positive thinking people. Listen to motivation programs. Read self-help books. Repeat affirmations daily. Order Michele's singing affirmation Albums. Michele wrote and recorded the singing affirmation music for this Action Program. I asked her to write and record a song on Action in Kuala Lumpur. At the time she knew no locals however she found a studio wrote and recorded the song and had it to me in 24 hours. That is Action. She has many albums. All great singing affirmations. Sing along with her, it's a wonderful way to add positive energy to your emotional self. (www.MicheleBlood.com)

By doing what I am suggesting your ideas will grow inside of you, then one day, pow, you'll automatically move into Action and your idea will move into form. Henry David Thoreau told us that when he said, "If a person will move confidently in the direction of their dream, and endeavor to live the life they have imagined they will meet with success, unexpected in common hours."

Thoreau was right. Mentally look after the idea and one day it will just happen. Action is the expression of an impression. When you mentally work on your big ideas the Action becomes automatic, you'll not be able to stop it. The Action comes from you which causes a reaction. The reaction comes from the universe. The Action meeting the reaction alters your conditions, circumstance, and environment which produces your result, your creation.

Permit me to share a wonderful story with you. It's a true story which happened to some very nice people in Northern Ontario, in Canada. The story is about a dirt-poor prospector who, day after day, month after month, year after year, would leave his home and his family to go prospecting for gold. There were times when they had next to nothing to eat. And when this man's wife or son voiced concern about the future the man would assure them, they need not worry, that the day would come, and they'd have wonderful times together when he found his gold mine. He was a man of great faith, but he was also a man of Action. He imagined himself with his gold mine and he would continually go out looking for it. He was a prospector. It was the week between Christmas and New Year's Day. At that time of year in Northern Ontario in Canada the snow is several feet deep and its bitter cold, freezing cold. It is predominantly a Christian community so being Christmas very few people work. Most folks lay around home. It's a time to be with the family.

Now although I have never checked this out, I feel fairly safe in saying there were babies born that week. In that cold, snow-swept town the babies didn't care what the occasion was or what the weather was like, the time had elapsed, the baby arrived, mum gave birth. The time also arrived for this man's idea to be acted upon. No one prospected for gold in this area between Christmas and New Year's. Anyone who did or even suggested that they were going to were probably considered insane. Nevertheless, this poor prospector called his partner and said, "It's time, we must go," and off they went.

Just outside of town the snow was so deep they were only able to venture a few feet off the main highway/ standing a few feet off the main road in freezing temperature and deep snow the poor prospector said, "This is the place." They went far beyond what any right-minded gold prospector would consider sensible with their drilling, however it was at that very place between Christmas and New Year's that the poor prospector and his partner became the extremely wealthy, multi-million dollar owners of the Hemlo Gold Mines. One of the richest gold mines ever found. It was at dinner one evening that Paul Larch told me that story.

You see the poor prospector who became the wealthy owner of the Hemlo mines is John

Larch, Paul's father. They were good, decent, nice people. If you met them, you would be happy it happened to them. Paul has told me that he just knew his dad would find a gold mine. He knew it because his dad kept telling him he would find it. From the time he was a little boy that's all Paul ever heard. And as Paul said, "Dad believed he would." It was that belief over the years that fueled the idea, the image. He impressed such great energy upon his subconscious mind for so long he moved himself into the vibration he had to be in to attract what he attracted. The image within John Larch became so explosive it had to be acted upon. Christmas, cold snow, none of that mattered. He had to act on the idea. The Action was automatic. It was the expression of an impression.

Do you have an idea big enough to keep you enthusiastic for years? John Larch did. A benefit which came to John as great as the gold mine is the faith, he instilled in his son Paul; the can-do attitude Paul was raised with. John Larch was a very rich man before he ever struck gold. He had and he gave his son what gold will not buy. Get your thinking right. If it is on the wrong track fix it. Remember, what you don't fix your children inherit.

Possibly the largest stumbling block any of us will face is the belief that something truly wonderful will happen in our life. It seems to be fairly easy for a person to believe that great things can happen to others but not to them. If you are caught up in this trap, I would suggest that you analyze the creative process. You will see we all have the tools for greatness. I have personally been studying the lives of successful people for over 30 years. Although these people come from varied backgrounds there is one factor which remains constant. The creative process which produces the results in their lives. Their results were preceded by an Action which was automatic. It was the expression of the thoughts and the ideas which had been impressed upon their emotional mind. Over a period of time they became what they thought about. The thought always propels action. You see, the bottom line is obvious when you become quiet and think. Every movement you engage in is an Action. Action is something you are already involved in. The trick in life is to control the Action, to create the type of explosive Action which causes us to find our gold mine. That is what all the big producers do.

I recently spent a weekend with Sam Kalanack. Our discussions resulted in me flying to Montreal to have another meeting with him. I would fly to the other side of the globe to spend a couple hours with this man. Sam Kalanack understands the importance of big ideas followed by explosive action. He is one of the truly big thinkers in the world today. Most people will not even give serious thought to certain ideas because there are obvious facts which would prevent the manifestation of the idea. Sam said, "If the idea is big enough the facts won't matter." Isn't that great? Think of it, if the idea is big enough the facts won't matter. Dr. Dennis Kimbrough from Atlanta, Georgia is one of the most effective public speakers I have ever heard. He has recently released "Think And Grow Rich: A Black Choice" which he wrote with Napoleon Hill. Dr. Kimbrough is a great thinker.

People like Sam Kalanack and Dr. Kimbrough used to be people I would read about but could not relate to. One day the idea settled in my mind, people like that who do great things were no different than I, I should get to know them. That idea grew because I kept feeding it. Eventually that idea had to be expressed in Action. Today I am like those men because I think I am, and I now know many of the world's great thinkers. You are like the great people that you read about. Take Action, go on and meet them. The more of these people you get to know the more you will see that you are alike, the better you will feel about yourself. The better you feel about yourself the more confident you will become. The more confident you become the easier it will be for you to move into Action on great, big, explosive ideas and solve the inherent problems that come with them.

Dato' Resham Singh, the director of engineering for Malaysia Airlines, had this to say about self-confidence. Remember and repeat this, it is something everyone should hear and understand. "When we feel confident about ourselves, we know we can solve the problems, or at least put them into perspective, and remind ourselves of our abilities when things aren't going well."

So, don't worry about what might happen when you explode into Action on your big idea. Whatever happens will be what must happen for your idea to move into form. Now, let's get busy. I'll bet your idea calls for ACTION!

For More Programs
https://www.proctorgallagherinstitute.com/

The Power of Meditation

Practicing Meditation forms the most important part of our work in becoming peaceful, happy, and connected to our Divine Presence. Michele Blood here. I wanted to add a couple more chapters that I know will assist you with your Success.

I was on a beach in Sarawak East Malaysia, and as I sat down to meditate, I was gazing the waves, and I became one with the waves I was watching. I was the wave. Here I was in Malaysia, working and creating programs with the great Bob Proctor and I was open and receptive to the Divine realizing the waves were me, and I was gone. The Eternal did indeed meditate me. Some people who are runners have had a similar experience. It is sublime and beautiful. Time stops.

The purpose of this chapter is to give you tools that will change your life by changing your thoughts. If that's true, then why speak about meditation which is meant to stop thoughts? Well, if we desire to move ahead and have success and good health flowing, we must continue to vibrate at faster and higher frequencies. The Divine Holy Light, which is our Higher Self, is the only true vibration. So of course, when we are going into the silence, we can connect with our true self and vibrate at higher frequencies. This is why I have what I call heart glow. Through meditating with focus on my heart chakra, the Divine within me has been activated. It is sublime. It is not always easy to begin to silence our mind, but it can be achieved. We have to practice tapping into that which sustains all of life.

The power of meditation is often overlooked. If you wish to truly connect with your Higher Self, then this chapter on meditation will assist you to look more deeply. This chapter will teach those who have never meditated before and will remind those who do practice meditation – its awesome power. When we practice meditation, we are consciously connecting, in the silence, to our Higher Power.

Although there are many ways taught to achieve silence through meditation practice, I will share with you some ideas that will meet your needs very nicely indeed.

I love to meditate in water, in nature, or on a beach; however, when we are meditating at home, I find it is best to create our own space where we will meditate. Clean this area well, as this will release old energies, because when we meditate it is best to have clean energy. Buy a brand-new mat on which to sit. Light a beautiful candle, as you can use the candle flame to focus your attention. A candle *does* bring good energy into your space as does traditional incense. A flower or a lush green plant is also good. If you do not live alone, ask your roommate or partner to please respect that this is your special place. Of course, to sit outdoors on the earth or on a beach is always energetically cleansing, but when at home, always designate a special place to meditate and meditate alone.

Meditation is not meant to make you sleepy; it is a focused practice. Visualization exercises are ok to do in bed as you can then flow into a positive sleep, filled with pictures that you can take into your dream time however meditation is not for relaxation, even though you will feel more harmonious. It is a very focused practice.

Once you have your meditation space prepared and cleaned, sit down on your mat, lotus style if you can, sit up straight, arms out to your sides and breathe in through your nose deeply, hold it and then exhale slowly through your mouth. Keep doing this until you feel peaceful. As you are now sitting peacefully, place your attention centered somewhere between the eyes and a little above. Next, take some word that is powerful to you, and you will know if it is powerful to you when you try some words out. LOVE, BLISS, GOD, SPIRIT, BEAUTY are good options. Ponder the word you choose. Some of my mantras are, *As a wave is one with the ocean, I am One with God, As a ray of sun is one with the sun, I am one with God, I Love God,* or *God's Grace is flowing through me, I am now a clear instrument for God's Grace,* or AUM. Use only one power word if that suits you better. You do not have to be religious to do this. Meditation is about focus and connection as a means to strengthen your mind. Replace the word God with Love if this feels more comfortable to you. I also love to listen to some Mozart because I find this keeps my mind still.

As you're sitting and focusing on your power word, Love, Heart, etc., your thoughts *will* wander off. When this happens gently refocus your mind back to the same mantra or word. Feel no impatience with yourself or frustration. No matter how many times your mind wanders, bring it back to that one word.

If you do this simple method, eventually, you will find that intruding thoughts will cease, and you will be able to sit quietly in a peaceful state. It may take days, or it may take months to acquire this steadiness of mind, but it will come if you have patience and are consistent.

At first, do not attempt to remain quiet for more than ten minutes or so unless you feel like it. After a couple of weeks, meditate for twenty minutes, and so on until you can sit comfortably for much longer periods. We are doing this to have a conscious realization of our unity with Spirit or to make contact with God. Keep it simple. KISS – "Keep It Simple and Spiritual," and remember to smile as we wish to bring a happy vibration to our meditation. I call smiling my *Happy Meditation*.

After ten to thirty minutes of meditation, and after you have achieved that feeling of peace, joy, and unity with the Universe, give thanks, get up, and go about your day. Please do this twice a day early am, and I love to also meditate at sunset and midnight when all is so quiet.

Even if you are agnostic, look at meditation as physicians do. It has been documented that people who meditate regularly have low blood pressure and generally are healthier, happier human beings. So, do it even if the word God is not your thing. Put a smile on your face as you sit down to meditate, as this does help your mind find peace. Do whatever you can to put yourself into a happy mindset before you sit down.

As mentioned, this chapter is a simple way of learning to practice meditation. Before we truly experience real silence, we are all only practicing meditation. But every time we do this, we do raise our consciousness, even if we do not realize it. In time, we will feel better and clearer, as well as less clogged or stressed.

Please do not begin this practice with an overly serious tone. Focused? Yes, but not so serious. Oscar Wilde said, *"Life is too serious to be taken seriously,"* so lighten up! Focus your attention and feel happiness and gratitude. This way, it is a simple and easy way to begin to practice, but do not underestimate its power. If you do not at, first feel any connection or peace of mind, that's fine. Just having the intention to consciously connect and feel the presence of God will eventually create peace, joy, harmony, and everything good will begin flowing your way.

WHY?

Because at least for a few minutes a day, you have chosen to get out of the way and let God in. As you delve into longer meditations and find a way that suits you best -and there are many different ways to learn meditation- your life and health will radically change for the better. Oh, yes, it will.

If you are having a hard time with your meditation practice, do not give up, and allow these loving and all-wise words by the great soul Paramahansa Yogananda to assist you: *"Your trouble with meditation is that you don't persevere long enough to get results. That is why you never know the power of a focused mind. If you let muddy water stand still for a long time, the mud will settle at the bottom, and the water will become clear. In meditation, when the mud of your restless thoughts begins to settle, the power of God begins to reflect in the clear waters of your consciousness. You will become a smile millionaire."*

Yogananda's books were my first lessons in meditation. I highly recommend you read, "Autobiography of a Yogi." I must have read it twenty or more times. Yes, let us become Smile Millionaires! Always remember to smile sincerely and breathe. Life is magical, oh yes, it is! Say right now:

Life Is Magical, and I Am Magical

Intuition

Intuition is part of *consciousness;* however, it is not pure consciousness. Developing our Intuition is vitally important if we wish to be free and KNOW that we KNOW. Logic has nothing to do with Intuition, nor does so-called *common sense.*

As we melt away the ice of duality, we can then tap deeply into the Power of our Intuition, where we are always clearly guided. With this guidance, our life becomes a glorious, happy, and purposeful experience. Whenever we are doing mind practices to bring more clarity and positive emotion, such as meditation and affirmations, our minds become clearer, we are happier, and our Intuition becomes very clear. People with strong Intuition are invariably happy souls because they can trust that they are guided from on high.

When we understand what Intuition is as opposed to an emotion we are feeling, our life will dramatically change. We will be guided. Our higher self will be speaking directly to us. We will know whom to speak to, when to speak to them, where to go and where not to go. This is so profoundly important for any soul to become FREE. We will be genuinely, Divinely guided. So please study this and begin with a few simple tools. Meditation practice, time, and advice when followed are all that's required to help us tap into the Power of our Intuition.

Intuition is so beautiful, simple, and profound. We will experience spiritual growth, and it will assist all areas of life, including our career and purpose. Intuition is the Infinite Intelligence speaking directly through us, to us!

Intuition means we are IN TUNE with God.

It doesn't matter what we choose to call God. We can call it our Magical Being, Spirit, Love, Higher Self, or Infinite Intelligence. When we are awake to our Intuition, we are awake and in tune with God. Duality is gone for a small amount of time, and we are unified. All the knowledge and creative ideas that have ever existed are totally available to us when we take the time to stop and listen. This is great as well for writers, or anyone in life. It's so important because when we are *in tune,* our creativity flows, and we don't have any blocks. *Yes, no more writer's block!*

While we are speaking of writer's block, here is a quick bit of advice to help you in your writing and creating. Profound studies and insights into how the brain operates have been made in the last few years. One of them is that it is essential to creative flow to keep the body well hydrated.

Even when the brain is dehydrated by only 10%, our brainpower diminishes by 30%. So, sometimes you might think you have writer's block, and you might *simply need water,* so stay hydrated.

Remember that Intuition is your soul directing you to all the good and all the success in your life. Please understand creative visualization, which is sometimes referred to as guided meditation, is an excellent practice to clear the mind from all the gunky thoughts out there. We literally become clogged. It is like ice surrounding the body, and we must melt away that ice to become clear.

Two of the most powerful ways to achieve this are to have regular physical exercise and daily meditation. Meditation helps clear the mind so that we can allow our Intuition to be clearly 'heard'. In a guided visualization, we learn how to relax the mind and allow someone else to speak to us and to guide us; we start focusing on what we *do want* to manifest into our magical lives. What is also recommended after a guided visualization is simply to be still. Learn how to breathe deeply, relax, and focus the mind. It is best to do this sitting up. This is especially true if you have not done any sort of visualization or guided meditation before. It takes a bit of practice to quiet the mind, and a visualization program is a great place to start.

Remember to inhale through your nose, hold it, and exhale slowly through your mouth. Just keep breathing. When we learn to stop thought, it feels that our higher voice is knock, knock, knocking, and at last, we can open the door. When we don't slow down and become quiet, we can't hear the knocking to open the door where all the answers are waiting to guide us to our next level of consciousness, success, and happiness. When we are silent, this awesome Power can be heard or felt speaking to us and through us. We must learn to be still long enough so we can hear and feel our Intuition. Also remember the importance of breathing, of gently focusing on our breath.

Intuition is not a strong emotion because when we feel emotional, it is usually our old thoughts and habits. Strong emotions are old paradigms. Old paradigms are our old thinking, old tapes in our mind being triggered by a situation in our human experience.

Intuition is that still, small, quiet voice. It's a knowingness. So, when we have a lot of emotion involved, it's usually not going to be our Intuition. Emotions are not feelings; they are the ego. Intuition doesn't seem to have any emotion, and yet it does feel peaceful. It's just a thought that silently comes to us—a quiet knowingness and guidance. When we have that *knowingness,* we have peace of mind and trust. It's simply beautiful. It's Mystical!

A Mystical experience is Divine Union; it is God speaking through us, and that is also Intuition. Our Higher Self is on duty. A psychic experience is all the different thoughts that we are picking up from the collective unconscious. What is the collective unconscious? The collective unconscious holds all the thoughts and emotions from all the people in our area of the world, and we tap into this cacophony of... well, mainly rubbish - *and you thought all that stuff you kept thinking were all your own thoughts.*

How do we know if something we are thinking is really our own thought? Well, this is not important. What is important is that you know whether it feels good or bad. If the thought feels bad NEXT IT!!

People become confused between the two experiences that occur in different dimensions, so let's now discuss Mysticism and psychic experiences. As we just discussed, Intuition is the Infinite directly speaking to us. It is a beautiful and magical power that we can all access and tap into when we pause to listen. A psychic experience is when we tap into other people's thoughts. As a common example. You think of a friend and call them, and they say they were just about to call you. We are all psychic, but that is not Intuition. When we use our Intuition, which is our Mystic connection to Spirit, now that is *real* Power. That's Mysticism. You do not need another person telling you about your future. YOU CREATE YOUR OWN FUTURE! Please know that you are much more powerful when you tune into the Mystical which is your Higher Self, and not the psychic part of you, as the Mystic message is directly from the Infinite, rather than that of other people's thoughts.

You are then totally one-to-one with Infinite Intelligence, *which can never be wrong.* You don't need to go through anyone else. Remember it's all about clarity. It's so important to be clear. What's also important to know is when we are not clear, because some people *don't know* that they *don't know,* and that is disempowering and somewhat sad. So, another reason why it is so important to dispel the fog, the clog from our minds, is so that our consciousness will be clear, which will then allow our Intuition to flow through to our conscious awareness.

When we are taking a shower, the water cleans our aura. Aura isn't just some hippy talk. It's now proven. Neuroscientists are proving that we do have a vibrational oscillation around us, and this vibration *is* in fact our aura or ethereal body. When that is blocked, nothing can flow.

Ideas don't flow smoothly, and we aren't able to make clear decisions. So, it's important to use all our tools of the mind to become clear. We don't want to be around people who have muddy minds and think negatively because their advice is not to be trusted as it is fear-based. I know that when we are communicating with other people if those around us are clear, we are not going to be manipulated by other people's fears or false judgments.

Did you know that everyone is intuitive?

It's not some great gift bestowed only upon special people. Everyone has intuitive abilities. It's just that sometimes we are clogged. We are living in a fog, and we must dispel that fog to let our intuitive powers flow through. Some people might say to someone, *"Oh, that person's really psychic."* Well, everyone's psychic. We all have a sixth sense. We can all pick up on the energies that are happening beyond the physical, that is no big deal. But oh, the Power of tuning in to our Intuition is beautiful and can be trusted. Listen to your heart, not your head. Now we know that we never need to be afraid of what life has to offer if we are looking inward with Spirit because we will *know* that we are always Divinely guided. All we have to do is stop and listen.

Please use your Intuition. Learn to meditate and use creative visualization. Learn to be still. Be on your own more often. Turn off the TV and be still. It's essential to clear the mind. Get rid of the muck. Be out in nature as much as possible. When our minds are clogged, we cannot think clearly, and often we are not even consciously aware of this clogging. Anytime we are feeling fear and not experiencing true joy in our hearts, that is the time we know to stop, breathe, and begin to do something different. Maybe go to see an uplifting movie, take a walk in nature, or meditate. Have beautiful natural plants and flowers around you because they help clean your air and give you pure oxygen and good energy.

So, tune into life from within...

About Bob Proctor

Bob Proctor, author of bestselling books and programs globally, is a world-renowned transformational, expert teacher. Bob is also the world's number one expert on how the Law Of Attraction really works. Bob Proctor is renowned for getting the very best out of both people and businesses. Bob's goal has always been to help others learn what it would take to meet their goals and show them how to tap into their endless potential.

In 1961, Bob Proctor started studying "Think and Grow Rich" and it transformed his life. Bob listened to Earl Nightingale's condensed recording of the book thousands of time. Then, Bob worked shoulder-to-shoulder with Earl Nightingale at Nightingale-Conant from 1968 to 1973, before leaving to start his own personal development company.

Bob has developed many strategies over the years which helped him to show others how they can succeed in things that they previously thought they couldn't, whilst helping people to develop the skills that they needed to achieve success and is considered the world's foremost expert on the human mind.

To get more information about Bob Proctor's courses and besting selling products go to:

https://www.proctorgallagherinstitute.com/

About Michele Blood

Michele Blood is a successful, multi-talented lady. Michele was a successful songwriter and rock singer in Australia and after a near-fatal car accident, while in the hospital with many serious injuries, she created positive Affirmation Songs which not only healed her body but also took her to worldwide success. These Affirmation songs affect the left and right hemispheres of the brain. Lyrics, the left hemisphere, and melody and music, the right hemisphere so the new, positive messages go straight to the subconscious mind. This is why millions of people worldwide have downloaded her Affirmation Power songs. These songs cover healing, success, money, joy, confidence and they uplift the person immediately.

In addition to creating Magnet To Success™ products and seminars worldwide, her public Mystical Success Events have been held in over 26 countries. Michele has co-written and created over 80 books, music CDs, audio programs, TV shows, and videos on positive thought, mind transformation, and meditation.

Her latest work is a truly powerful and magical App. www.MagnetToMoneyApp.com

Bob Proctor, from "The Secret", who wrote many programs with Michele says,
"Michele Blood is truly a special person. For over three decades, I have made serious study of the mind and how to live a full and balanced life. I have taught tens of thousands of people around the world how to properly utilize their God-given potential, and then along came Michele Blood. She had a very positive impact on my life, for which I am truly grateful! She made me aware of unique methods for realizing more power by effectively combining affirmations and music. Invest in her entire

library and let this petite powerhouse show you a fast and effective way to enjoy more of life's rich rewards. I enthusiastically introduce Michele Blood and her wonderful work to every audience. Order her material today! Share Michele and her MusiVation™ discovery with your world; they will thank you with sincere gratitude."

Jack Canfield, Author of "Chicken Soup For The Soul", says,
"Michele Blood's energy is incredible. She is a walking billboard for what she teaches, a high-vibration being. I thank her for the work she is doing in the world. I love it, and she's right about the two hemispheres of the brain working together through her Affirmation Power Music Songs. Everything moving in harmony. Beautiful."

www.MicheleBlood.com

The New Paradigms Complete Audiobook & eBook For Only $20.00

Imagine delving into the captivating audio version of this book with Bob Proctor himself speaking. The secrets of the Law Of Attraction will be revealed like never before. With nearly 3 years of dedication invested in creating and producing this audio program by Bob Proctor and Michele Blood, you can rest assured that every moment of this program is crafted with the utmost care and precision, tailored specifically for your success.

If you would like the complete audiobook and eBook versions of this book at a discount since you have this printed book just go to:
www.NewParadigmsAudio.com

On the checkout page click the link that says "Have a coupon? Click here to enter your code" and enter the following coupon code on the checkout page.

More Love (Is the code)

AVAILABLE NOW!
THE WORLD'S FIRST MANIFESTATION VIDEO BOOK

Recalibrate Your Consciousness And Life To Success

www.ManifestationVideoBook.com

The Most Anticipated Manifestation App Is At Last Here!
The Magnet To Money App
For iPhones & iPods

Read 5-Star Reviews Here:
<u>MagnetToMoneyApp.com</u>

You Can Become A Magnet To Money

- 💲 Faster Than Any Other Manifestation Method
- 💲 Recharge Your Morning with 8-Minute Wealth & Success Meditations
- 💲 Fall Asleep to Words of Prosperity and Love
- 💲 Increase Your Wealth & Good Fortune for 2023!
- 💲 Have True & Lasting Success Through Higher Consciousness
- 💲 Transform Your Mind to Attract Wealth

You Are a Magnet to Money - Let This App Show You How

Scan This QR Code

THE MYSTICAL EXPERIENCE™
www.TheMysticalExperience.com

**Vibrate at a higher frequency.
Ignite Your True Unlimited Potential and Experience Success in Life Through Transformation of Consciousness with this life changing platform.
Since 2003 transforming thousands of lives.**

How can we transform our lives?

Through transforming our consciousness. Can we do this alone? Yes, however it is a very difficult path to do alone. Here at the Mystical Experience, you are prayed for every single day and sent transmissions of Light Energy (Shakti).

Here in the Mystical Experience™ it is our goal and positive intention to strip away old paradigms of false beliefs and become one with our true Higher Self. And hence our Divine Destiny is at last revealed in all its glory! There is much given through this membership in Divine vibrational energy transmissions, exercises, videos and more.

Do you wish to have harmony, happiness and fulfilling success? You can wake up to who you truly are. ALL things are possible. The natural evolution for all sentient beings, and that means YOU, is ENLIGHTENMENT! If you feel you want evolution in all areas of your life, then watch our FREE videos at...

www.TheMysticalExperience.com

MY MIND GOALS

I, _____, am so happy and grateful for my Beautiful, Rich, Healthy, Enlightened Life. All of this that I write has manifested into my consciousness and into my life experience.

MY FINANCIAL GOALS

I, _____, am so happy and grateful for my Beautiful, Rich, Healthy, Enlightened Life. All of this that I write has manifested into my consciousness and into my life experience.

MY SOCIAL GOALS

I, _____, am so happy and grateful for my Beautiful, Rich, Healthy, Enlightened Life. All of this that I write has manifested into my consciousness and into my life experience.

MY FAMILY GOALS

I, _____, am so happy and grateful for my Beautiful, Rich, Healthy, Enlightened Life. All of this that I write has manifested into my consciousness and into my life experience.

MY TRAVEL GOALS

I, _____, am so happy and grateful for my Beautiful, Rich, Healthy, Enlightened Life. All of this that I write has manifested into my consciousness and into my life experience.

MY SPIRITUAL GOALS

I, _____, am so happy and grateful for my Beautiful, Rich, Healthy, Enlightened Life. All of this that I write has manifested into my consciousness and into my life experience.

MY CAREER GOALS

I, _____, am so happy and grateful for my Beautiful, Rich, Healthy, Enlightened Life. All of this that I write has manifested into my consciousness and into my life experience.

MY GLOBAL GOALS

I, _____, am so happy and grateful for my Beautiful, Rich, Healthy, Enlightened Life. All of this that I write has manifested into my consciousness and into my life experience.

MY MATERIAL GOALS

I, _____, am so happy and grateful for my Beautiful, Rich, Healthy, Enlightened Life. All of this that I write has manifested into my consciousness and into my life experience.

MY PHYSICAL GOALS

I, _____, am so happy and grateful for my Beautiful, Rich, Healthy, Enlightened Life. All of this that I write has manifested into my consciousness and into my life experience.

www.ingramcontent.com/pod-product-compliance
Lightning Source LLC
Chambersburg PA
CBHW050236120526
44590CB00016B/2111